CAMBRIDGE UNIVERSITY PRESS

CAMBRIDGE ENGLISH Language Assessment
Part of the University of Cambridge

CAMBRIDGE OFFICIAL PREPARATION MATERIAL

Kid's Box

Updated Second Edition

Student's Book 5

American English

Caroline Nixon & Michael Tomlinson

Language summary

	Key vocabulary	Key grammar and functions	Phonics
Welcome to our ezine page 4	School subjects: *art, computer studies, English, French, geography, history, math, P.E., science, Spanish* School: *competition, dictionary, exam, language, lesson, prize, study, subject, timetable*	*Like/love* + *-ing* / nouns, *'d like* + infinitive Simple present questions and short answers: *Do you live close to your school? Yes, I do. / No, I don't. Is it on Thursday? Yes, it is. / No, it isn't.*	Consonant sounds: "j" (*jump, orange*) and "ch" (*cheese, lunch*)
1 Time for TV page 10	Time: *after, a quarter after, half, o'clock* TV shows: *cartoon, comedy, documentary, music video, news, quiz show, sports, weather* TV: *action movie, channel, episode, series, turn on* Adjectives: *amazing, bad, boring, exciting, funny, good, interesting*	The time: *What time is it? It's a quarter after one.*	Vowel sound: "yoo" (*usually, music*)
History Cartoons page 16			
2 People at work page 18	Jobs: *actor, artist, cook, dancer, dentist, doctor, farmer, firefighter, mechanic, manager, nurse, pilot, reporter, secretary, soccer player, sports commentator, swimmer, teacher, writer*	Plans, intentions, and predictions: *going to*	Short vowel sound: "er" (*manager, actor, treasure*)
Science Teeth page 24		**Review** 1 and 2 page 26	
3 City life page 28	City life: *airport, bridge, castle, fire station, gym, hotel, museum, playground, police station, post office, prison, restaurant, road, stadium, street, taxi/cab, theater, zoo* Directions: *across, corner, down, past, left, right, straight ahead*	Directions: *Go down / across (Green Street), Take the first/second/third street on the left/right, Go straight ahead, Turn left into (Blue Street), Turn right at the corner, Stop before you get to the (river), Walk past the (playground), What's at the end of (the street)?, be lost* Prepositions: *across from, behind, between, next to*	Consonant sounds: "s" (*socks*) and "sh" (*gosh, machine*)
Geography Cities page 34			
4 Disaster! page 36	Disasters: *earthquake, hurricane, iceberg, lightning, storm, tsunami, volcano* Verbs: *break (leg), catch fire, cut, destroy, drop, erupt, fall down, hit, hurt, lose* Months	Past progressive and simple past: *I was having a picnic when it started to rain. What were you doing when the teacher saw you?*	Stressed syllables
Geography The earth's surface page 42		**Review** 3 and 4 page 44	

Welcome to our ezine

Show what you know! What school words can you remember?

Listening **1** 02 CD1 Listen and check (✓) the school words you hear.

2 03 CD1 Listen again. Who said it?

1 Did you have a good vacation? Dan.
2 What's an ezine?
3 It's an internet magazine.
4 Can we write about sports and computers?
5 Let's write our first ezine on our school.
6 See you outside school at four o'clock.

3 Answer the questions.

1 What are the children's names?
2 Where are they?
3 Where's the poster?
4 What's an ezine?
5 What's the prize for?
6 What can they write about?

LOOK

Nice to meet you.

4 Read and answer.

Kid's Box is an exciting new ezine for young people. Let's meet the writers, Dan, Alex, and Maria. They all go to the same school. It's called "City School."

Alex

I'm eleven years old. I always ride my bike to school. I sometimes have breakfast with the school breakfast club before my classes. I love playing soccer and basketball. I'm also interested in computers. I'd like to write about sports and computers in the ezine.

Dan

I'm ten. I live in the country outside the town, so I catch a bus to school every morning. I like singing and music. I love playing the guitar and the piano. I'd like to write about music and clothes in the ezine.

Maria

I'm ten. I live close to the school, so I walk in every day. I have lunch in school with my friends. I love drawing and taking pictures, so I want to put my pictures in the ezine and write about the natural world.

1. What's *Kid's Box*?
2. Who's interested in computers?
3. Which school do they go to?
4. How does Alex go to school?
5. How old is Dan?
6. What would Dan like to write about?
7. What does Maria love doing?
8. Who's the oldest, Alex, Maria, or Dan?

5 Listen and say the name.

04 CD1

Who lives close to the school?

Maria does.

6 Ask and answer.

Do you live close to your school?

No, I don't.

~~live / close to school~~
lunch / home
play / musical instrument

like / sports
read / magazines
use / the Internet

Now think of some more questions.

Reading **7** Read and think. What's your favorite school subject? Why?

http://www.cambridge.org/elt/kidsbox/ezine

Kid's Box Ezine!

home | reports | games | world | email

★ For our first ezine we went around our school to find out more about what we learn.
We all study these school subjects: math, English, science, music, P.E., art, and computer studies.

Kid's Box reports Our School

a

Older students have to study more school subjects and take important exams.

b

We study a second language. We can choose French, German, or Spanish.

c

We use the dictionaries in the school library to help us understand new words.

d

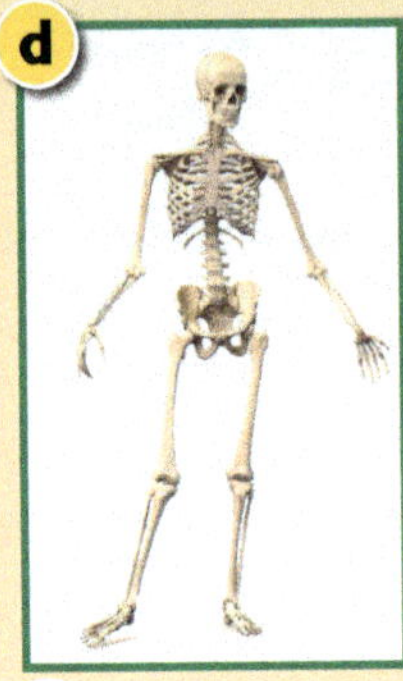

Science is an important subject, so we do it every day. This year we're learning about plants and the human body.

e

In our geography classes we learn about different people and their countries.

f

The best subject is history. We love learning about the past!

We all agree that the best thing about school right now is the new ezine competition. We all want to win that prize!

science | history | geography | language | school subjects | exam | dictionary

8 05 CD1 Listen. Repeat the word and say the letter.

1 History.

History. That's "f."

9 Read again and say "same" or "different."

1 At City School they all study music.
2 Older students take important exams.
3 They can choose a second language.
4 There are dictionaries in the school library.
5 They study science every day.
6 They think history is better than geography.

10 Listen and say the subject. (06 CD1)

1 A lot of people think the capital of Australia is Sydney, but it isn't. It's Canberra.

Geography.

11 Read and choose the right words.

1 We study the past in **science / geography / history.**
2 French, Spanish, and German are **languages / exams / math.**
3 When we don't understand a word, we can use **a book / a dictionary / art.**
4 We study plants and the human body in **math / P.E. / science.**
5 We learn about people and countries in **geography / computer studies / music.**
6 Teachers sometimes find out what we know by giving us **subjects / computers / exams.**

12 Listen and match. Check and sing. (07 CD1)

a

b

Because school is cool, it's where we go
From Monday through Friday, I'm sure you know.
We study and we play, that's what we do.
We do it in the morning and the afternoon!

c

1

d

I really love (1)geography,
And I enjoy (2)history.
I like to study (3)science, too!
My favorite subject in the afternoon.

Before lunch we have (4)music,
And then (5)computer studies,
And on Wednesday we do (6)sports.
That's a class that is too short!

e

f

And I like to do (7)languages,
Spanish, French and Japanese.
A lot of words in the (8)dictionary,
For me to study and to read.

g

h
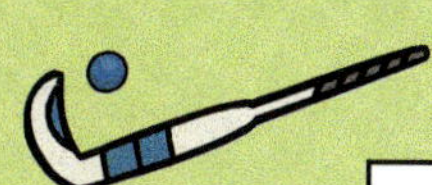

13 Read about the school words. What are they?

With this subject we can learn to talk to people from another country.

In this class we learn about plants and the human body.

When we study this, we learn about different countries and people.

We use this to learn new words.

14 Write three more definitions. Ask and answer.

With this subject we can learn about numbers and shapes. What is it?

Is it math?

Yes, it is.

15 Focus on phonics

Jill likes geography and German,
Her favorite subjects in school.
Charlie likes French, eating lunch,
And jumping in the pool!

Speaking 16 Play the game. Guess it in ten.

MY SCHOOL SCHEDULE

	Monday	Tuesday	Wednesday	Thursday	Friday
8:00–9:00	history	math	music	science	math
9:00–10:00	English	computer studies	geography	P.E.	
recess					
11:00–12:00	art	science	science	French	English
12:00–13:00		music	computer studies	history	geography
lunch					
14:00–15:00	French	P.E.	history	English	computer studies
15:00–16:00	geography		math	art	French

Is it on Thursday? Yes, it is.

Is it before lunch? No, it isn't.

Is it at three o'clock? Yes, it is.

Is it art? Yes, it is.

Writing 17 Write your school schedule.

Joke Corner

Why doesn't the elephant like computer studies?

He's afraid of the mouse.

DIGGORY BONES

12 CD1

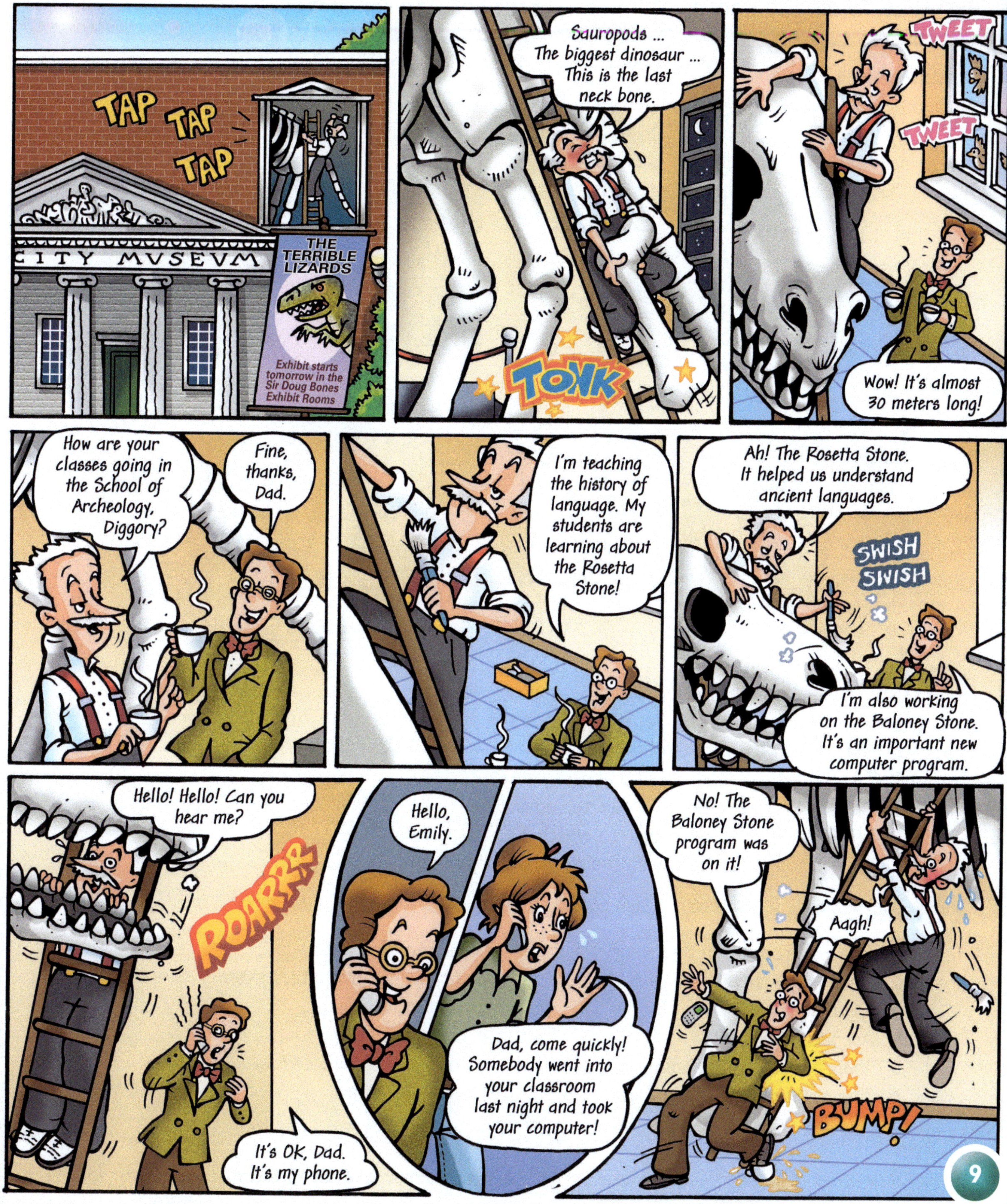

1 Time for TV

Show what you know! What TV words can you remember?

Listening **1** 13 CD1 Listen and check (✓) the TV words you hear.

2 14 CD1 Listen again. Say "yes" or "no."

1 The children are in the supermarket at the beginning of the story. (No.)
2 *Fun time* is on TV at ten after four.
3 They want to watch a show about animals.
4 The kids arrive home at a quarter after five.
5 The kids go to Alex's house to watch TV.
6 Mr. Nelson wants to watch the same show as them.

3 Read and match.

1 The children are in the library
2 They leave the library
3 *Fun time* is on TV1
4 *Animals* is on TV2
5 The children arrive home
6 The golf finishes

a at ten after four.
b at twenty-five after seven.
c at ten to four.
d at twenty after four.
e at a quarter after four.
f at five to four.

LOOK

It's **a quarter to** four. It's **a quarter after** four.

4 Read and label the clock.

ten after	five after	twenty-five to	a quarter to

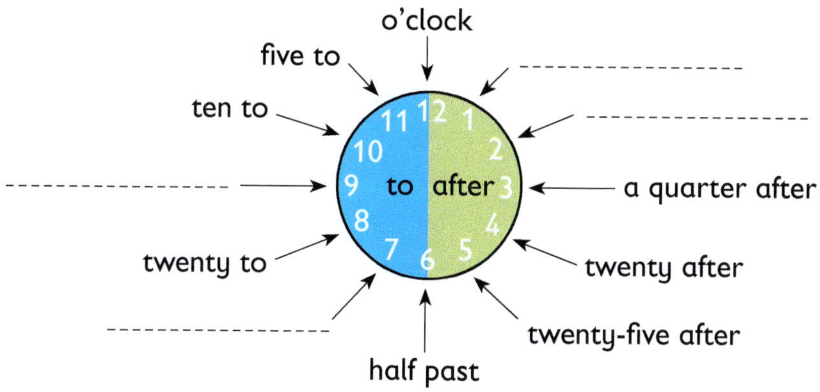

5 Do the actions.
Tell the time.

What time is it?

6 Look at the clocks. Ask and answer.

What time is it?

It's a quarter after one.

1 – b

7 15 CD1 Listen and say the letter.

1 … I have lunch at a quarter to one every day.

a

8 Play the game. Ask and answer.

Reading 9 Read and think. What's your favorite TV show? Why?

http://www.cambridge.org/elt/kidsbox/ezine

Kid's Box Ezine!

home | reports | games | world | email

Kid's Box reports TV

Most children love watching TV. So today's ezine is about TV. There are a lot of channels on TV and many different kinds of shows.

a

Cartoons are moving pictures. Children love them. They can be short shows or complete movies. They're usually funny.

b

We watch the weather to find out if it is sunny, rainy, windy, or cloudy. What's the weather like today?

c

A documentary is a show that tells us about our world. It can be about animals, history, or geography.

d

A comedy is a funny show that makes us laugh. What's your favorite comedy?

e

The news is about all the things that happen in the world. It is on TV every day. What time is the news on in your country?

f

A quiz is a kind of competition. One person asks others a lot of different questions. The winner is the person with the most points.

g

The most popular sports shows in our country are baseball, basketball, and tennis. What are they in your country?

h

We watch a series in parts. These parts are called "episodes." You can sometimes watch an episode every day.

cartoon | weather | documentary | news | comedy | series | sports | quiz

10 16 CD1 Listen. Repeat the word and say the letter. 1 Quiz. Quiz. That's "f."

11 Read again and answer.

1 Which show is in episodes?
2 Which show is funny?
3 Which show is a kind of competition?
4 Which show can be short or a complete movie?
5 Which show can tell us things about animals?
6 Which show can tell us to take an umbrella with us?

12 Listen and say the show.

17 CD1

1 Goal!

Sports.

a cartoon | b weather | c sports | d documentary | e news | f music videos | g comedy show | h quiz show

13 Choose words to talk about the different shows.

interesting exciting boring good bad funny amazing

I think quiz shows are more interesting than the weather.

I think music videos are the best.

14 Listen and complete. Check and sing.

18 CD1

I don't like TV, I don't like it much,
But there are some shows that
I sometimes watch.

On channel one at ,
There's a really good documentary
About animals and where they live,
What they do and what they eat,
And on channel four at ,
They put on a great cartoon.

At one o'clock and then at ,
They show the news and then the weather.
They're not my thing, they're not for me,
But I like the sports at .
But what I like, what I love the best,
Are the action movies, more than the rest.
They're on at ,
And at , but I want more.

15 Read and complete.

news turned on waited ~~four~~ arrived past

Tim and Jen went to the park last Saturday. They ran on the grass, played with a ball, and went on the swings. At ten to (1) four_______ they sat down because they were tired. They saw a newspaper on the bench. They opened it at the TV page and looked to see what was on the different channels. Tim wanted to go home and watch *Friendly* at half (2) ______________ four. They went to the bus stop and (3) ______________. The bus didn't come until a quarter after four. They (4) ______________ home at twenty-five to five, ran into the living room, and (5) ______________ the TV. The show wasn't *Friendly*, it was the (6) ______________. They looked at the newspaper again. It was an old one! They showed *Friendly* on Friday, not on Saturday.

16 Focus on phonics

20 CD1

The students usually use computers
At the university on Tuesdays.
But today they're at the museum,
Playing beautiful music!

Speaking 17 Ask your friend.

Questionnaire

1	How often do you watch TV?	*Three times a week.*
2	What's your favorite show?	
3	What kind of show is it?	
4	What day's it on?	
5	What time's it on?	
6	Why do you like it?	

Writing 18 Write about your friend.

Peter watches TV three times a week. His favorite show is ...

Joke Corner

21 CD1

What's the worst time to play soccer?

When it's five to one.

DIGGORY BONES

23 CD1

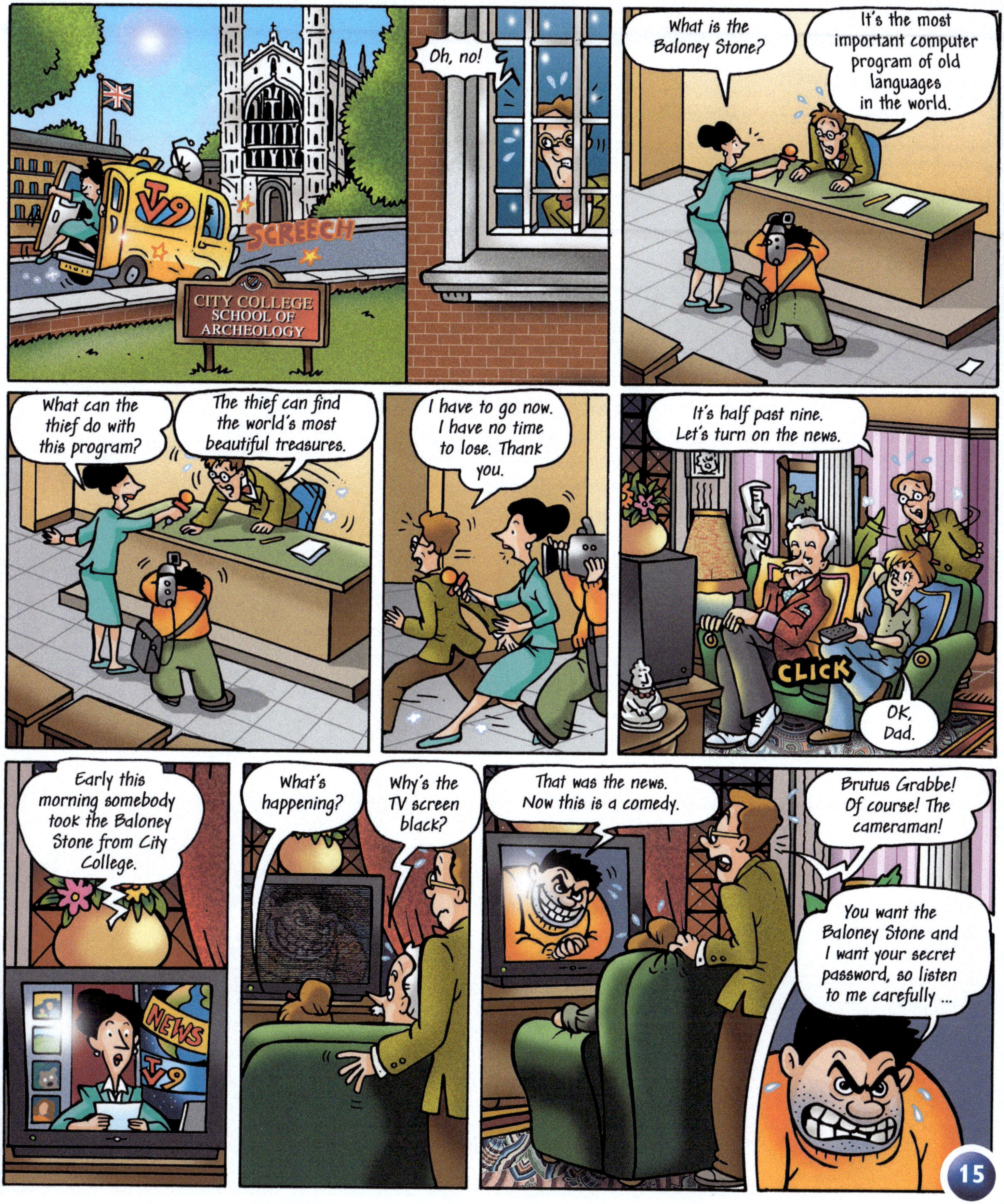

History Cartoons

FACT: *The Simpsons* started in 1987. It's the longest-running cartoon series.

1 Ask and answer.

Do you watch cartoons? Who's your favorite cartoon character?

a

2 Look and say.

Do you know the names of these cartoons? Which characters are in them?

b

c

3 Read and answer.

Movies and cartoons are made of a lot of different images. In movies the different images are called frames, and in cartoons they are called cels. In a movie there are usually 24 frames per second, and in a cartoon there are 12 cels per second. Our eyes do not see the space between each frame or cel.

1 How many frames do you need for 15 seconds of movie?

2 How many cels do you need for one minute of animation?

There are lots of different ways to make cartoons. The first cartoons were made using hand-drawn pictures. Today, some cartoons are drawn using cel animation. For these, artists have to draw pictures on clear plastic. This means that to change the cels they only have to redraw the parts of the picture that move.

Other cartoons, such as *Wallace and Gromit*, use models. Artists move the models and take a photograph. They have to take a lot of photographs!

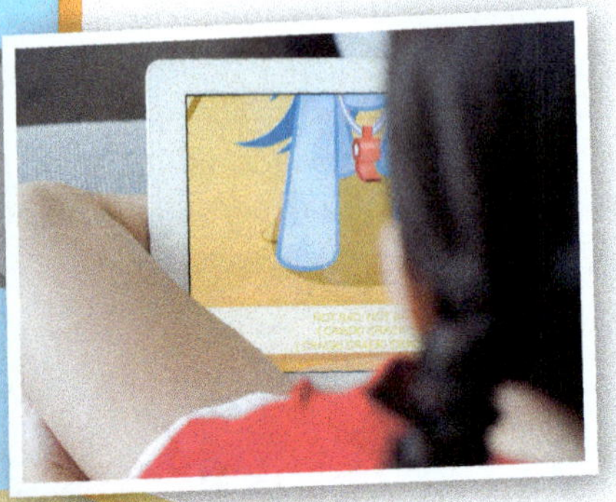

3 Which method of making a cartoon do you think would take the longest? Why?

These days, most cartoons are made using special techniques with a lot of help from computers. Now, anyone can make a cartoon using cartoon-making websites. You could make a cartoon, too.

4 Can you think of an idea for a cartoon?

4 Listen and choose the answer.

1 The first important cartoon character was
   a) Felix the Cat. b) Shrek. c) Mickey Mouse.
2 A lot of cartoon characters are
   a) teachers. b) animals. c) flowers.
3 Walt Disney made the first cartoon in color in
   a) 1910. b) 1932. c) 1956.
4 In the 1990s cartoonists started to use
   a) color. b) computers. c) sound.
5 *Shrek* won a prize for the best
   a) animated movie. b) character. c) music.
6 There are a lot of fantastic new animated movies every
   a) week. b) month. c) year.

5 Listen again and put the information on the timeline.

computers sound color ~~*Felix the Cat*~~ *Shrek* *Toy Story*

1920s *Felix the Cat*
1928 ____________
1932 ____________
1990s ____________
1995 ____________
2001 ____________

Project Make a flipbook cartoon.

You need:

- 2 sheets of heavy paper or thin cardboard
- A pencil and scissors
- Crayons or markers
- A big stapler or a big clip

How to make the flipbook:

1 Cut each sheet of thin card into six squares.
2 Number the cards from 1 to 12 and draw the same bounce line on all 12 cards. Then draw a ball on the bounce line to the left of the first card. Draw the same ball on each card just to the right of the one before.
3 Put the cards in order. Staple one side.
4 Now flip through your cartoon book.

2 People at work

Show what you know! What jobs can you remember?

Listening **1** 27 CD1 Listen and check (✓) the jobs you hear.

2 28 CD1 Listen again. Complete the sentences.

1. They're looking at an exhibit on ______________ .
2. Dan thinks he's going to be a ______________ .
3. Maria thinks she's going to be a ______________ .
4. Maria hopes the ______________ isn't going to burn down.
5. Alex's going to be a ______________ .
6. They're going to write about famous people's ______________ .

3 Read and order the words.

1. write about / What / for our ezine? / are / we / going to
2. going to / a nurse / be / when I'm older. / I'm
3. a doctor. / going to / Alex / be / isn't
4. The school / isn't / burn down. / going to
5. win / prize! / We're / that / going to
6. do / you / What / tomorrow? / are / going to

LOOK

I'm **going to be** a dentist.
Alex **isn't going to be** a nurse.
What **are we going to write** about?

4 Listen and order. Check and sing.

29 CD1

a She's going to help them all,
And work in schools … ☐

b They're going to do their best,
Then sleep and play. ☐

c They're going to do the job,
Then work all day,
Then sleep and play … ☐

d She's going to show the kids,
She's going to teach good rules. ☐

e They're going to do the job,
They're going to work all day. ☐

f He's going to do his best,
Then sleep and play … ☐

g He's going to do the job,
He's going to work all day. 1

5 Look and say. What are they going to do?

a

b

c

d

e

f

6 Correct the sentences.

No, she isn't going to wash her face.
She's going to brush her teeth.

a) She's going to wash her face.
b) They're going to go to a music festival.
c) They're going to turn on a computer.
d) He's going to play tennis.
e) They're going to watch TV.
f) He's going to wake up.

7 Ask your friend.

1. Where are you going to go after school?
2. Who are you going to see this evening?
3. When are you going to do your homework?
4. What time are you going to go to bed tonight?

Now think of some more questions.

Reading **8** Read and think. What's the most exciting job? Why?

http://www.cambridge.org/elt/kidsbox/ezine

Kid's Box Ezine!

home | reports | games | world | email

In today's ezine we're going to look at some interesting people and their jobs.

Kid's Box reports

Jobs

a

John Travolta is a famous actor. His movies include *Grease* and *Hairspray*. He is also a pilot. This is his hobby. He has five planes, and he can fly all of them.

b

People remember George Orwell because he was an important writer. Two of his most famous novels are *Animal Farm* and *1984*. He was also a reporter, and wrote for different newspapers.

c

When Mia Hamm was young, she was a soccer player. She scored more than 100 goals for the U.S.A. and won the Women's World Cup. In 1999, she started the Mia Hamm Foundation. It helps girls start playing soccer.

d

Jamie Oliver is a famous cook who also works on TV. In his show *Jamie's School Dinners*, he made children's school meals healthier.

e

Formula 1 is a car racing competition. It's a team sport. One of the most important people on the team is the mechanic. Steve Matchett was a Formula 1 mechanic. He had to repair cars during the race. Now Steve works as a sports commentator on TV.

f

Mrs. Barbara Blackburn was a secretary. She was one of the best in the world. She had a special typewriter, and she could type faster than any other typist. She could type 150 words in a minute. Amazing!

secretary | soccer player | actor | reporter | cook | writer | mechanic | pilot

9 31 CD1 Listen. Repeat the word and say the name of the person.

1 Cook.

Cook. That's Jamie Oliver.

10 Read again and answer.

1. What did the soccer player win?
2. What did the cook do in *Jamie's School Dinners*?
3. Why is the secretary famous?
4. What did Steve Matchett repair?
5. Who is a pilot and an actor?
6. What different jobs did George Orwell have?
7. How many of these people are on TV?

11 Listen and match. Say the job.

(32 CD1)

1 Good evening. This is Captain Bird speaking. Welcome aboard flight 241 from Dublin to London.

Pilot. That's "e."

a 

b 

c 

d 

e 

f 

12 Listen again and choose the right words.

(33 CD1)

1 The plane is flying to **New York / London / Paris**.
2 Bill brushes his teeth **well / badly / on Saturdays.**
3 The cook is making a **chocolate cake / carrot cake / cheesecake.**
4 Mr. Hamilton can get his car at **ten o'clock / half past nine / half past ten.**
5 The cowboy is **happy / hungry / cold.**
6 The reporter is going to interview a **soccer player / swimmer / basketball player.**

13 Play the game. Guess it in ten.

Do you work at the fire station?

No, I don't.

Do you wear a uniform?

Yes, I do.

14 Read and think. Ask and answer.

What's Teresa going to be when she grows up?

She's going to be a cook.

Teresa	loves making cakes and working in the kitchen.
Richard	loves studying science and the human body.
William	loves drawing and painting.
Helen	likes working with children. She loves reading them stories.
Robert	loves animals and going to the country. He's very strong.
Katy	loves playing with cars and building things.

15 Think about somebody you know who has an interesting job. Answer the questions.

1 Who does this job?
2 What's his/her job?
3 What does he/she do at work?
4 Why do you think it's interesting?

Now ask your friend the questions.

16 Focus on phonics

CD1 34

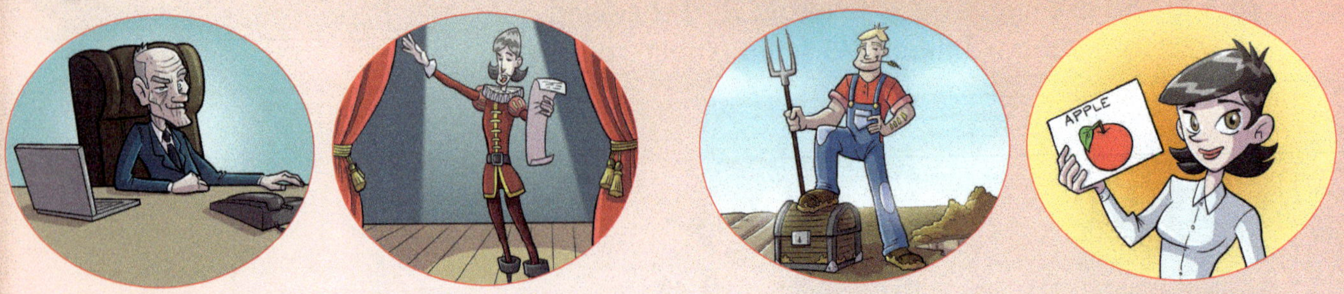

Manager, actor, swimmer, writer,
Older, taller, stronger, faster.

Farmer, teacher, doctor, dancer,
Treasure, picture, paper, answer!

Speaking 17 Ask and answer.

Writing 18 Write your plans for next week. Don't repeat any verbs!

On Monday after school I'm going to play
with my friends.
On Tuesday ...

Joke Corner

CD1 35

A man went to the doctor with bananas in his ears and a carrot in his nose. What did the doctor say?

He said, "You're sick because you aren't eating right."

DIGGORY BONES

37 CD1

Science Teeth

FACT: **People cleaned their teeth with wood and animal hair before William Addis invented the first toothbrush in 1780.**

1 Read and match.

a
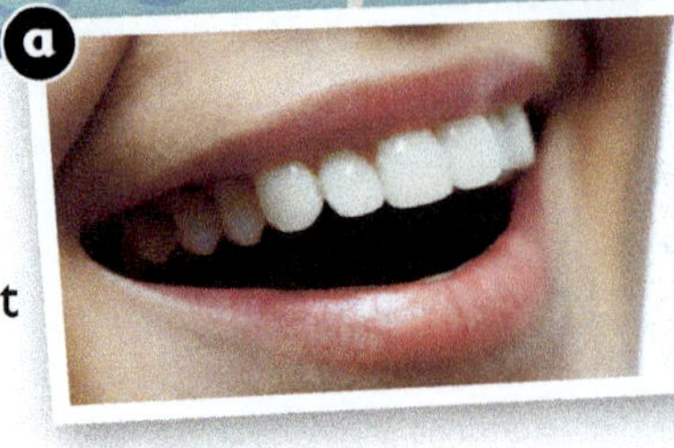

b
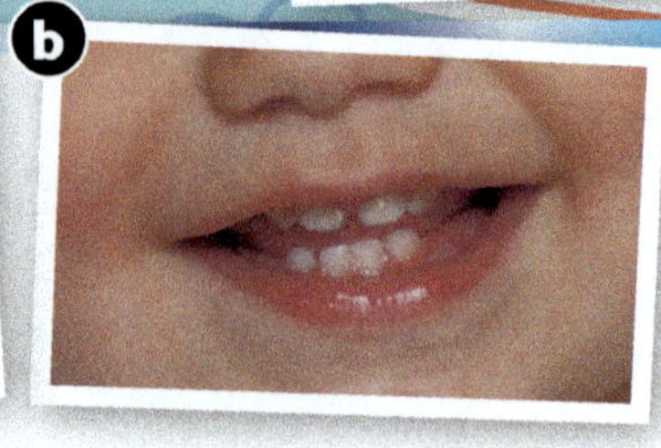

c
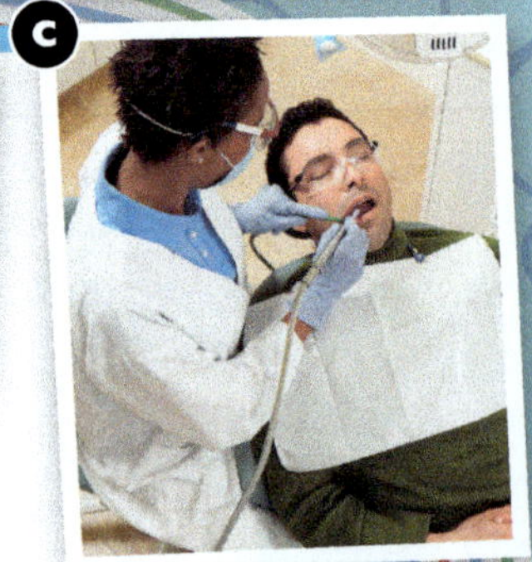

Our dentist

We start going to our dentist when we are very young because dentists help us take care of our teeth. Healthy teeth help us eat, speak clearly, and look good.

Our baby teeth

We get 20 baby teeth when we are between six months and three years old. Then we lose these teeth and get a permanent set of about 32 teeth.

Our permanent teeth

The first 28 permanent teeth appear when we are between six and 13. The final four molars, or wisdom teeth, usually come when we are between 16 and 21. Not everyone gets wisdom teeth. Do you know if your parents got theirs?

2 Read and label the diagram.

Our different teeth

We have four kinds of teeth, which do different things:

- We have eight **incisors** at the front of our mouths. They're the sharpest teeth because they cut our food.
- The four **canine** teeth are next to the incisors. They hold and tear food, so they have very long roots.
- Our eight **premolars** are behind our canine teeth. We use them to chew food, so premolars are flatter on the top.
- The **molars** are at the back of our mouths. Molars are much bigger than the premolars. Their job is to chew food into smaller pieces so it can be swallowed.

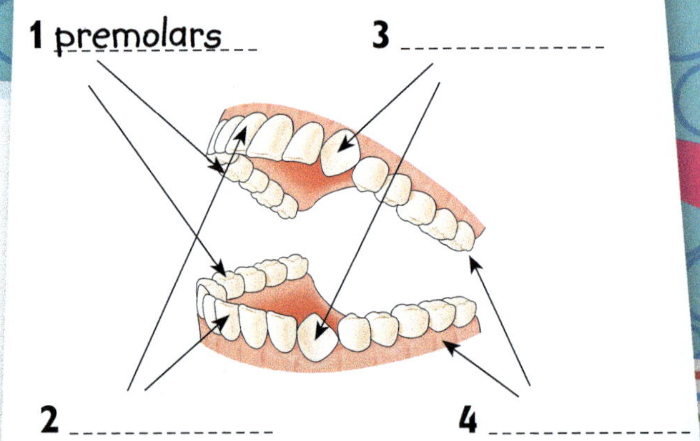

3 Match the sentences with the picture.

Tooth structure

A tooth has two parts: the crown and the root.

1 The **crown** is the part we can see when we smile or open our mouth.
2 We can't see the **root** because it is in the gums. It is about two-thirds of the tooth's total length.
3 The hard white part that covers the outside of the tooth is called the **enamel**.

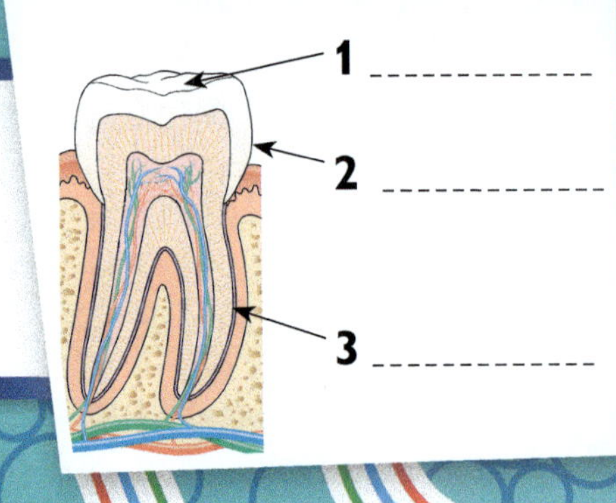

4 Read and complete.

healthy between finish ~~after~~ shouldn't before hungry brush dentist better

Tooth care

To have healthy teeth and gums, you must:

1 brush your teeth every day _after_____ meals and ______________ bed.

2 eat a good diet. You ______________ eat sugary foods ______________ meals. If you are ______________ , eat an apple, a banana, or a carrot.
Don't drink lemonade. Drink milk! If you eat between meals, ______________ your teeth when you ______________ .

3 visit the ______________ twice a year. A dentist can clean your teeth ______________ than you so that your mouth is ______________ .

5 Read and order the text.

How to brush your teeth

[ ] To finish, rinse out your mouth with water.

[ ] Always start and finish in the same place in your mouth. A good place to start is the outside of the back molars, which need the most time and brushing.

[ ] All of that should take two minutes.

[1] Brushing your teeth is very important. It cleans your teeth and gums, and helps against cavities.

[6] Then repeat all of this on your bottom teeth.

[ ] Lastly, don't forget the top of your mouth and your tongue.

[ ] Next brush the inside of your teeth and gums using the same circular movement.

[ ] When you finish the inside and outside of your top teeth, quickly brush along the chewing part of your teeth.

[3] Gently brush the back molars and gums using a small circular movement. Then move slowly around your mouth brushing all your teeth.

Project Do a dentist's experiment.

You need:

- A toothbrush
- Toothpaste with fluoride
- 2 eggs
- A bottle of white vinegar
- 2 clear plastic cups

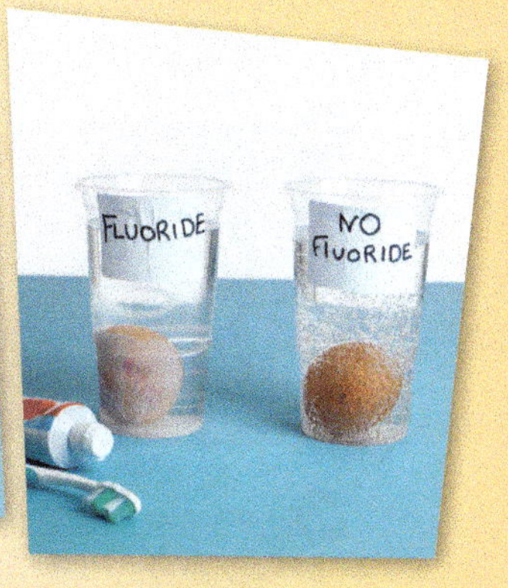

What to do:

1 Brush one of the eggs with fluoride toothpaste.

2 Put 10 cm of vinegar into both cups. Put the "fluoride" egg into one cup of vinegar and the other egg into the other cup of vinegar.

What happens:

Bubbles start to appear on one egg as the vinegar (an acid) attacks the minerals in the egg shell. Which egg do you think bubbles are going to appear on?

Review Units 1 and 2

1 Sarah is talking to her mother, Mrs. Smith. Read the conversation and choose the best answer. You do not need to use all the letters.

a Can we go out to the park?
b Yes, please. Can I phone Katy to see if she can come?
c My favorite comedy's on at twenty-five after five.
d I think it's about half past eleven.
e All right, then. Can I call Peter?
f Thanks, Mom. Can you hand me the phone?
g Which ones should I wear? My sneakers?
h Does Peter like history?

Example

Mrs. Smith: What time is it, Sarah?
Sarah: d

Questions

1 **Mrs. Smith:** What do you want to do?
Sarah: ---------------

2 **Mrs. Smith:** OK. Put your shoes on.
Sarah: ---------------

3 **Mrs. Smith:** Yes, the blue ones. Listen, do you want to go with a friend?
Sarah: ---------------

4 **Mrs. Smith:** I think Katy's studying for an exam this afternoon.
Sarah: ---------------

5 **Mrs. Smith:** OK. Call him and see if he wants to come, too.
Sarah: ---------------
Mrs. Smith: Here you are. Tell Peter to bring his bike!

2 Tell your friend the story. There is one example. It's morning. The boy is going to school.

3 Now write the story.

4 Play the game.

What are you going to do tomorrow?

Instructions

- Go around the board. Say the time and what you are going to do at that time.
- Think of a different activity for each time.
- To keep playing you have to remember the activity that goes with each time. If you cannot remember, then go back to START and wait for another turn.

That's a quarter to seven. Tomorrow I'm going to wake up at a quarter to seven.

That's nine o'clock. Tomorrow I'm going to wake up at a quarter to seven and go to school at nine o'clock.

3 City life

Show what you know! What city words can you remember?

Listening **1** 02 CD2 Listen and check (✓) the city words you hear.

2 03 CD2 Listen again. Choose the right words.

1 They arrive at **ten after two / twenty to three**.
2 They want information for their **ezine / school homework**.
3 They decide to visit a **bridge / museum** first.
4 They start outside the **station / school**.
5 They're lost because of problems with the **map / bus**.
6 Tower Bridge is **behind / across** the street.

3 Read and complete the sentences.

1 We have to go ___ this road.
2 We don't go across the river. We turn ___ here.
3 Now we're at a ___ .
4 I think we take the third street on the ___ , then walk ___ this park.
5 Let's go ___ .
6 It's just ___ the street.

LOOK

right · left · straight ahead · corner · past · across · along

4 Look at the map. Read the directions and answer.

1 Go up High Street. Take the third street on the left and stop after the river. What's on the right?

2 Go up High Street and turn right onto Blue Street. Turn left onto Low Road, and then go across Green Street. What's on the corner, on the left, across from the movie theater?

3 Go up High Street, and take the second street on the left. Walk past the playground. What's next to it?

5 04 CD2 Listen to the directions and answer.

1 Go straight ahead. Take the second street on the left. What's at the end of the street?

The river.

6 Play the game.

Go up the High Street and take the third street on the right. Go across Low Road, and it's next to the music store.

Is it the produce market?

Yes, it is!

7 Write the directions to (1) the bank and (2) the computer store.

Reading 8 Read and think. Is London an exciting city? Why?

http://www.cambridge.org/elt/kidsbox/ezine

Kid's Box Ezine!

home | reports | games | world | email

Kid's Box reports London

Yesterday we went to London and saw a lot of interesting places. Here are some of our pictures.

a

New Scotland Yard is one of the most famous police stations in the world. A king of Scotland lived in the first Scotland Yard.

b

This is the British Museum. There are six million objects here. One of them is the Rosetta Stone.

c

This is the new Globe Theater. The first Globe Theater was famous because William Shakespeare showed his plays there.

d

You can buy stamps for your postcards in the Trafalgar Square post office. They sold the first sticker stamps in this post office in 2001.

e

This is Brown's. It's a hotel and restaurant. It's the oldest hotel in London. Rudyard Kipling wrote *The Jungle Book* here.

f

London has six airports. This is Heathrow. It is the busiest airport in the world. 64 million people use this airport every year!

g

This castle is next to Tower Bridge. It's called the Tower of London. It looks beautiful now, but for many years it was a terrible prison. Many people died here.

h

This is a London taxi. It's called a black cab. Drivers of black cabs have to pass a test to show that they know all the streets in London.

taxi | hotel | police station | airport | restaurant | museum | castle | theater | post office

9 (05 CD2) Listen. Repeat the word and say the name of the place.

1 Castle.

Castle. That's the Tower of London.

10 Read again and correct these sentences.

1 You can see the Rosetta Stone at the Natural History Museum.
2 William Shakespeare showed his movies here.
3 They sold the first postcards here.
4 Brown's is a store and hotel.
5 London has seven airports.
6 London buses are called black cabs.

11 Listen and complete. Check and sing.

castle	zoo	restaurant	taxi
~~museum~~	station	theater	
Bridge	street	park	

Theater, movies,
Restaurant and hotel,
Museum, castle,
A story to tell.

I went to London,
To have a nice day.
To go to a museum and
The ________ for a play.

I saw Tower ________
And the ________, too.
Walked in the ________
And went to the ________.

I went to a ________
On the corner of the ________.
I sat outside and
I had something to eat.

I took a ________
Because it was late.
My train was in the ________.
It was half past eight.

12 Ask and answer.

cook	firefighter	manager
actor	bus driver	doctor
teacher	pilot	police officer

Who goes to work in a restaurant or hotel?

A cook.

13 Look at the map. Ask and answer.

Where's the theater?

It's between the gym and the library.

14 Think of a place you know. Give directions how to get there from your school. Can your friend guess?

Go out of the door, turn left, take the second street on your right, and walk past "Flower's Restaurant." What can you see?

Is it the stadium?

Yes, it is.

15 Focus on phonics

Sally: I need some socks, Scott.
Scott: But there aren't any stores at the bus station, Sally.
Sally: Look! What's that?
Scott: Gosh! It's a sock machine!

Speaking 16 Find ten differences.

In the first picture there's a green bus, but in the second picture there's a red bus.

1

2

Writing 17 Choose one of the pictures and write about it.

The first picture is of a town.
I can see ...

Joke Corner

What starts with "p," ends with "e," and has thousands of letters in it?

A post office.

DIGGORY BONES

Geography Cities

FACT **Istanbul, in Turkey, is the only city that is on two continents. It's called the "bridge between Asia and Europe."**

1 Can you name these cities?

a 

b 

c 

d 

2 Read and answer "true" or "false."

1. During the Stone Age, cavemen started fishing.
2. Cities started growing where there were markets.
3. Cities stopped growing because of the Industrial Revolution.
4. Four thousand people lived in Mohenjo-Daro 40,000 years ago.
5. London is smaller than New York.
6. New York has more skyscrapers than Tokyo.

3 Read and order the events.

a) London was the biggest city in the world. ☐
b) People started building cities. ☐
c) New York was bigger than London. ☐
d) Cavemen started farming. 1
e) Tokyo is the biggest city in the world. ☐
f) Rome was the most important city in the world. ☐

Why did the first cities start?

During the Stone Age, cavemen started farming. As they got better at farming, they started growing more food than they could eat. They bought and sold the extra food in markets. Cities started growing around these markets.

Living in cities made people feel safe. People often lived close to castles and built walls around their houses. Two hundred years ago, cities started growing much faster. This was because of the Industrial Revolution. People went to work in the cities because there was more money.

Where were the first cities?

Mohenjo-Daro in the Indus Valley, in Pakistan, was one of the first cities. It was built more than 4,000 years ago. About 40,000 people lived there. If we look at a map of Mohenjo-Daro, we can see the streets were straight and that there were a lot of houses and big buildings.

About 2,000 years later, the biggest city in the world was Rome. It was the capital of the Roman Republic and Empire for a thousand years. About a million people lived there.

London was the first city to have more people than Rome. It was the biggest city in the world between 1831 and 1925. Then New York grew bigger. Now the biggest city in the world is Tokyo, but New York has more skyscrapers.

4 In groups talk about a city you know.

a) What can you find in your city? Make a mind map.

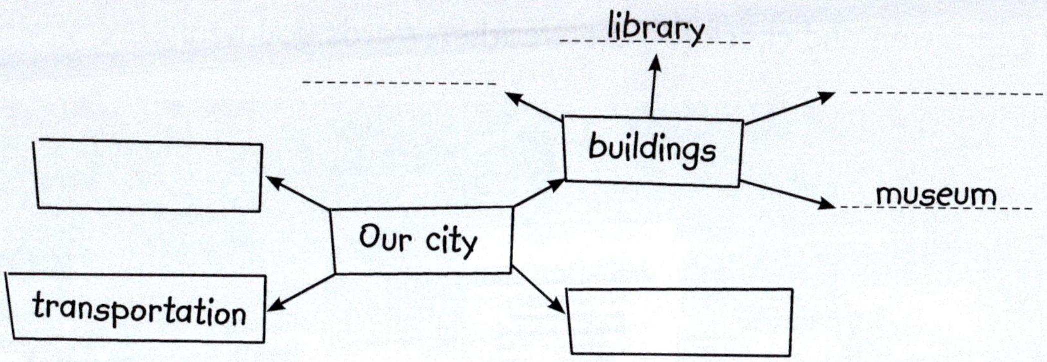

b) Make two columns in your notebook and write a list of the "good" things and the "bad" things about your city. Talk about why you think they are good or bad. How can you make the bad things better?

Our city	
Good	Bad
park	cars

Project

Design a new city.

Work in groups. Ask and answer.

- What do you want in your city?
- What do you need in your city?
- Where do you want to put parks, schools, houses, stores, markets?
- How can people go from their home to school, to stores, and to work?

How to make your city:

1. Make a map of your city on a big piece of cardboard.
2. Write the names of the places in your city on pieces of colored paper. Put them on your map to show where you want them.
3. Think of a name for your city and tell the other groups about it.

4 Disaster!

Show what you know! What weather words can you remember?

Listening 1 13 CD2 Listen and check (✓) the weather words you hear.

2 14 CD2 Listen again. Who said it?

1 Now we have a great project for our ezine … disasters! (Alex)
2 We decided to sail to this small island for a picnic with my dad.
3 When we were sailing to the island, the sky went dark.
4 The radio was on, but we weren't listening to the weather. We were listening to music.
5 We were walking up the beach, looking for somewhere safe to stay, when lightning hit the boat.
6 It was really exciting when the helicopter came to get us.

LOOK

Were you **listening** to the weather on the radio?
We **weren't listening** to the radio.
We **were listening** to music.

3 Read and match.

1 They were sailing to the island
2 They were waiting on the island
3 The radio was on,
4 When the storm started,
5 They were walking away from the boat
6 They were getting warm

a they were waiting on the island.
b when the lightning hit it.
c when the sky went dark.
d when the reporter arrived.
e when the helicopter appeared.
f but they weren't listening to the weather.

4 Listen and complete. Check and sing.

15 CD2

swimming | skating | sitting | eating | ~~walking~~ | climbing | playing | sailing

What were you doing when the storm began?
When the lightning hit and the water ran.
Where were you when the rain came down?
On the mountain, at the beach, in the forest or the town.

I was walking up the mountain,
He was ________ over the lake,
We were ________ in the park,
She was ________ a piece of cake.

They were ________ in the river,
He was ________ on the ocean,
She was ________ up a wall,
I was ________ under a tree.

5 What were you doing when these things happened? Write three sentences.

- hurt your knee
- teacher saw you
- dropped your cell phone
- cut your hand
- lightning hit the tree
- started to rain
- shoe fell off
- mother took a picture of you
- started to feel sick
- lost your watch

I was having a picnic lunch when it started to rain.

6 Play the game. Guess it in five.

What was I doing when it started to rain?

Were you having a picnic lunch?

Yes, I was.

Reading **7** Read and think. Which was the worst disaster? Why?

http://www.cambridge.org/elt/kidsbox/ezine

Kid's Box Ezine!

home | reports | games | world | email

Disasters sometimes happen, as we recently found out. We decided to find out about some famous disasters.

Kid's Box reports Disasters

a

This ship is called the Titanic. On April 14, 1912, it was traveling across the Atlantic Ocean when it hit an iceberg. They couldn't see the iceberg because of the fog.

b

The Hindenburg was one of the biggest airships ever built. On May 6, 1937, when it was arriving in the U.S.A., it caught fire. People think this happened because lightning hit it during a storm.

c

Hurricanes are very dangerous storms with strong winds. The worst Atlantic hurricane in history was the Great Hurricane in 1780, from October 10 through 16.

d

When a volcano erupts, it throws hot liquid rock and gases into the air through the hole at the top. When Krakatoa erupted on August 26, 1883, it made the loudest sound ever heard.

e

On November 1, 1755, an earthquake hit Lisbon, in Portugal. The ground moved for ten minutes. The earthquake destroyed most of the buildings in the city.

f

On December 28, 1908, a tsunami hit Messina, in Italy. The enormous wall of seawater was about ten meters high. How high do you think the seawater is in this picture?

tsunami | hurricane | volcano | earthquake | iceberg | storm

8 17 CD2 Listen and say "yes" or "no." Repeat or correct.

1 The tsunami was on December 28, 1908.

Yes. The tsunami was on December 28, 1908.

9 18 CD2 Listen and repeat the chant.

January, February, March,
April, May, June,
July, August, September,
October, November, December.

10 19 CD2 Listen and say the months.

1 It's sunny and windy. There are a lot of red apples on the trees …

September.

11 Ask and answer.

It's February. What can you see?

Some children are reading comic books. They're sitting in their living room next to the fire.

12 Cross out the extra word.

1 What were they to doing on Wednesday, November 13?
2 There was a many bad storm on May 31.
3 They couldn't see because of was the fog.
4 Why was do he running?
5 The lightning hit the my car on August 19.
6 My birthday was in the January.
7 The fire did started on June 29.
8 In Antarctica there's a very lot of ice.

13 Read the notes and write about what happened.

Friday March 13 was a terrible day for Jane. What happened?

when / go / downstairs / put / foot / on / toy / car
fall / down / break / leg
ambulance / come / take / to / hospital
when / nurses / carry / Jane / into / hospital / drop / her
now / Jane / in / hospital / with / broken / leg / and / broken / arm

When Jane was going downstairs, she put her foot on a toy car.

14 Focus on phonics

20 CD2

There's a **bad storm** with **thun**der and **rain**,
An **aw**ful **earth**quake is **shak**ing a **train**.

A vol**ca**nic e**rup**tion **makes** a **ter**rible **sound**,
While a **dan**gerous **hur**ricane **blows** all a**round**!

Speaking 15 Complete the questions. Ask and answer.

What were you doing at …		Name ______	Name ______	Name ______
1	8:45 yesterday morning?			
2	4:15 ______ ?			
3	______ last Sunday morning?			
4	______			
5	______			

Writing 16 Write your diary for last week.

Monday
I was watching TV when John came over. It was a great surprise! We played on the computer, and he stayed for dinner.

Joke Corner

21 CD2

What place is in this joke?

The Red Sea.

DIGGORY BONES

23 CD2

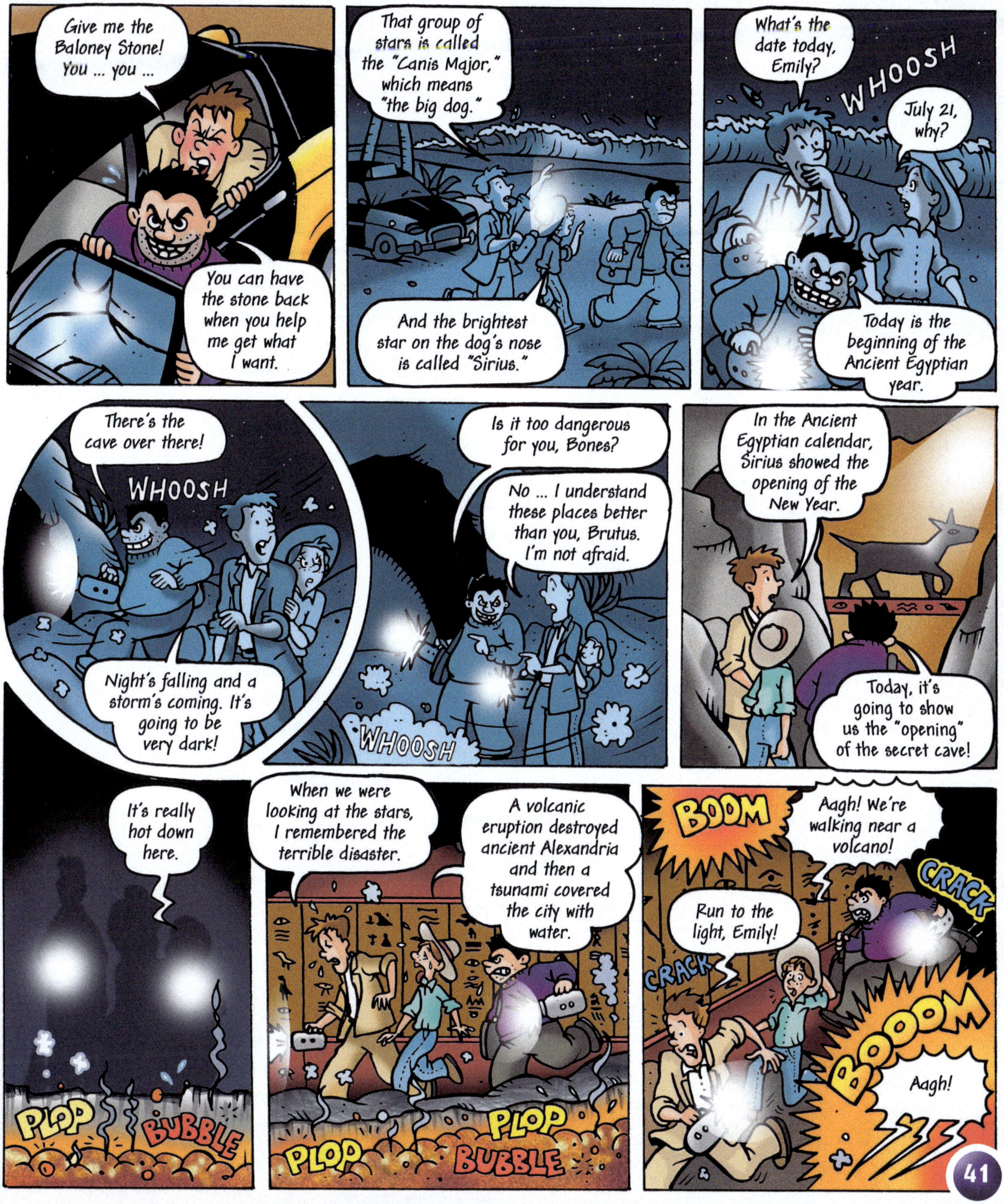

Geography The earth's surface

FACT: **The word *volcano* comes from the Roman god of fire, Vulcan.**

1 Read and answer.

1 What is the name for the outside of the earth?

2 What are plates?

3 What does the Richter scale measure?

4 Where are most tsunamis?

2 Read again and choose a title.

a) Plates and bowls

b) Natural disasters

c) Wave problems

3 Complete the sentences.

1 Two of the worst natural disasters are ______________ and tsunamis.

2 The ______________ of the earth is a solid rock layer called the crust.

3 The crust has different parts that are called ______________ .

4 People use a seismometer to ______________ how strong an earthquake is.

5 A ______________ is a series of enormous waves.

6 About ______________ out of every ten tsunamis happen in the Pacific Ocean.

A natural disaster is the name we give to something that happens because of natural forces and not because of the actions of people. Two of the worst natural disasters are earthquakes and tsunamis. They happen when land moves, and they're very frightening.

The outside of the earth is a solid rock layer called the crust. The crust has different parts that are called plates. The line where plates meet is called a plate boundary. Earthquakes and tsunamis often happen on or close to the plate boundaries.

Earthquakes

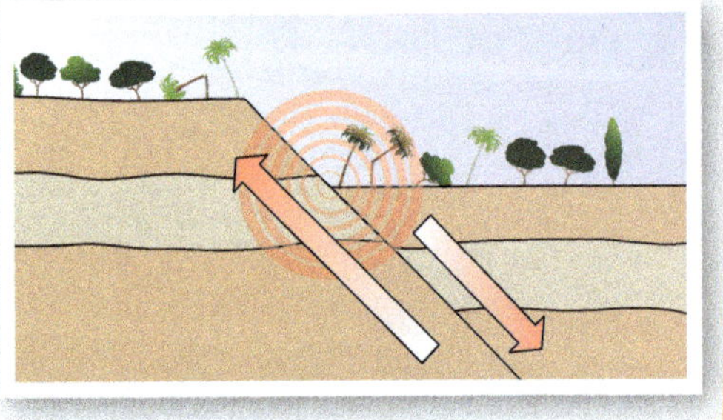

An earthquake is a sudden movement of the earth's surface. The plates under the earth are always moving slowly, but sometimes they stick and can't move until they move suddenly. This can cause an earthquake. People use a seismometer to measure how strong an earthquake is. A seismometer uses the Richter scale when it measures an earthquake. The Richter scale is numbered 0–10. Very bad earthquakes have a high number.

Tsunamis

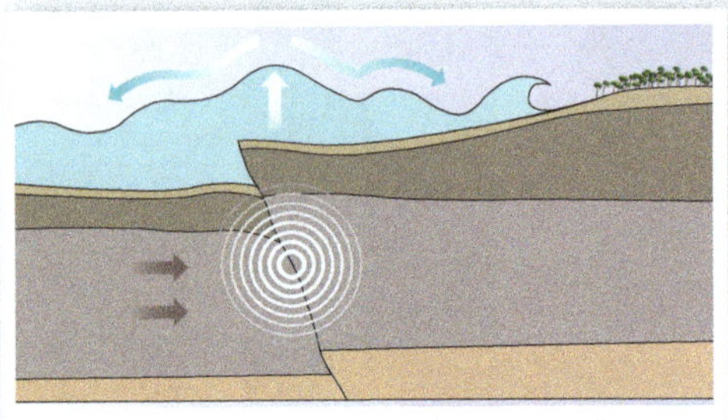

A tsunami is a series of enormous waves. Most tsunamis happen because of a big underwater earthquake. The earthquake must be over 6.75 on the Richter scale. About nine out of every ten tsunamis happen in the Pacific Ocean. Tsunamis are different from normal waves because they move a lot more quickly and the distance between one wave and the next is bigger.

4 Read and label the diagram.

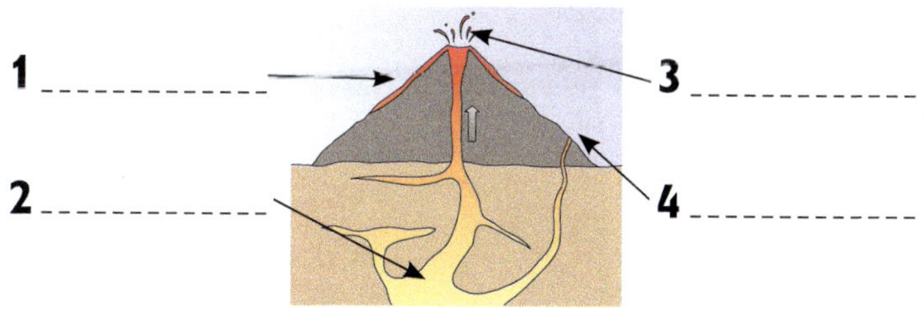

Volcanoes

A volcano is a mountain with a hole on the top. Volcanoes erupt when magma (liquid rock) from under the crust breaks through the crust. When magma reaches the earth's crust, it is called lava, but when it becomes cold, it forms rock. The bowl shape at the top of the volcano is called a crater, and the smaller holes in the side are called vents. The biggest volcano is Mauna Loa in Hawaii. It is about 10 km tall from the ocean floor to its top.

5 (24 CD2) Listen. What is Mount Saint Helens?

6 (25 CD2) Listen again and choose the answer.

1 Where is Mount Saint Helens?
U.S.A. / Indonesia / Australia

2 It was the worst eruption in **the world. / the U.S.A. / Indonesia.**

3 What was the date?
May 18, 1980 / March 18, 1980 / May 8, 1980

4 When did the volcano erupt?
7:30 / 8:00 / 8:30

5 How far into the sky did the cloud go?
9 km / 19 km / 90 km

Project Make a volcano.

You need:

- A water bottle
- Tape
- Cardboard (60 x 60 cm)
- Newspaper
- Flour
- A bowl
- Paint
- Scissors

How to make the volcano:

1 Cut the top of the water bottle off. Tape the bottle to the center of the cardboard.

2 Make newspaper rolls and balls to stick around the bottle.

3 Mix water and flour in the bowl to make glue. Tear the newspaper and put it into the glue.

4 Put the newspaper over the rolls to make the shape of the volcano. Don't cover the top of the bottle.

5 Wait for the paper and glue to dry completely. In the next class, paint your volcano.

Review Units 3 and 4

1 Read the letter and write the missing words.

Dear Aunt Petra,

I'm writing to tell you about the great time we ___had___ last weekend. I think Mom told you we were going to Manchester on Saturday. Well, we went to the stadium to see a soccer game, because Manchester United were playing against Liverpool. I really enjoyed it but Liverpool didn't (1)______________ . They (2)______________ 1–0.

On Sunday we spent the day exploring the city. We got lost because we didn't have a (3)______________ . No problem! We asked a police officer for (4)______________ and he showed us where to go. We visited the Lowry Museum, which had some interesting paintings by a famous (5)______________ from Manchester, L.S. Lowry. There is a picture of one of his paintings with the letter. Hope you like it.

Yours,

Jamie

2 Listen and check (✓) the box.

26 CD2

1 Where did Paul go yesterday?

a ✓ b c

2 What did they do first?

a b c

3 What did they do in the park?

a b c

4 What did they have for lunch?

a b c

5 What was the movie about?

a b c

6 How did Paul get to the airport?

a b c

3 Play the game.

Find your way home

Instructions

- Go around the board following the instructions. When you stop on a picture, spell the word. If it's right, roll again. If it's wrong, stop.

5 Material things

Show what you know! What materials can you remember?

Listening **1** 27 CD2 Listen and check (✓) the materials you hear.

2 28 CD2 Listen again. Say "yes" or "no."

1 The children go to a pet store. (No.)
2 The mice are made of milk.
3 The teeth are made of sugar.
4 The snakes are made of paper.
5 The spiders are made of chocolate.
6 Dan's afraid of spiders.

3 Read and choose the right words.

1 The shopping mall is made **on** / **of** brick.
2 The mice **is** / **are** made of white chocolate.
3 The teeth **is** / **are** made of sugar.
4 The snake is made of **rubber** / **bone**.
5 The small black spiders are **made** / **make** of fur.
6 The spider on Dan's shoulder **is** / **isn't** real.

LOOK

The mice **are made of** chocolate.
The spider **isn't made of** fur.
What **are** they **made of**?

4 Ask and answer.

What's the school made of?

I think it's made of stone.

a

b

c

d

e

f

g

h

5 29 CD2 Listen and check.

Is your new school bag made of leather?

Yes, it is.

That's "c."

6 Read and match.

1 This is my favorite hat. I can wear it every day because it changes with the weather. When it's raining, it has two pieces of plastic to cover my ears.

2 When it's cold, a special scarf that is made of fur comes out to cover my neck.

3 When it's sunny, I turn it inside out, and I have a sun hat that protects me from the sun. It has some sunglasses made of special plastic to protect my eyes.

a

b

c

4 These are my favorite shoes. I wear them on weekends. They are a lot of different colors.

5 When I touch one of the colors, the shoes change to that color. Look!

6 If I jump or drop the shoes on the floor, they bounce. The shoes can help me jump very high – up to two meters! This is because they are made of a special rubber called "bounce-a-lot." I'm going to bounce to the park. Goodbye.

d

e

f

7 Read again and correct the sentences.

1. The hat changes every day.
2. When it's raining, it has two pieces of plastic to cover his eyes.
3. The sunglasses are made of special rocks.
4. The shoes can help her swim.
5. If you drop the shoes, they dance.
6. The shoes are made of wood.

Reading **8** Read and think. What's the most important material? Why?

http://www.cambridge.org/elt/kidsbox/ezine

Kid's Box Ezine!

home | reports | games | world | email

Kid's Box reports Materials

Materials can be man-made or natural. We make man-made materials in factories. We get natural materials from rocks in the ground, animals, and plants. Here are some interesting things made of different materials.

a

Most houses are made of bricks, stone, or wood, but Edouard Arsenault used 12,000 glass bottles to build this amazing house.

c

d

Cardboard and paper come from trees. Cardboard is stronger than paper. This tower is made of thin cardboard, and the bridge is made of paper.

Gold and silver are precious metals. This car is made of 80 kilograms of gold and 15 kilograms of silver. You have to drive it very carefully!

b

e

Most animals have fur, but sheep have wool. We use wool to make clothes. This dress is made of wool. It has animal teeth and bones on it to make it beautiful.

A lot of things are made of plastic. Today we use plastic more than any other material in the world. We must recycle plastic. "Recycle" means use it again in a different form. This chair is made of recycled plastic.

f

wood | gold | glass | cardboard | paper | wool | metal | silver | plastic

9 30 CD2 Listen. Repeat the word and say what's made of it.

1 Glass.

Glass. That's the house.

10 Read again and answer.

1. Where do we make man-made materials?
2. How much gold is in the car?
3. How many glass bottles did Arsenault use to build his house?
4. Where does paper come from?
5. What does the dress have on it?
6. What does "recycle" mean?

11 Read and choose the right words.

1 Paper and cardboard are made from **wood / wool / metal**.
2 Gold comes from **animals / the ground / trees**.
3 Wood comes from **ground / trees / flowers**.
4 Fur comes from **trees / sand / animals**.
5 Glass is made from **leaves / sand / wood**.
6 Wool comes from a **sheep / cow / bear**.

12 Listen and order. Check and sing.

31 CD2

a This table's made of wood,
And that skirt's made of grass. ☐

b **From rocks, plants, or animals,**
Or from a factory. ☐

c This scarf is made of wool,
And I wear it when it's cold. ☐

d This chair is made of metal,
That bowl is made of glass. ☐

e Some things are made of plastic
That can be strong and hard. ☐

f This box is made of silver,
That watch is made of gold. ☐

g **Everything's material,**
Everything we see. 1

h Books are made of paper,
Their covers are made of
cardboard. ☐

13 Close your book. What can you remember from the song?

14 Play the game in pairs.

wood	metal	glass	plastic	paper
pencil				

15 Focus on phonics

33 CD2

Clare: It's time to take a break.
Dean: Let's sit on the chairs and eat our pears.
Clare: Great! But wait! Look behind that gate ...
Dean: Run, Clare! Those bears want our pears!

Speaking 16

Play the game. Choose words to make six sentences.

meet	~~knows~~	right	would	some	red	ate
sun	write	wood	read	sum	wait	sea
hour	bored	meat	pair	where	pear	hear
son	board	for	see	there	here	weight
their	four	nose	eight	our	wear	

My mom knows I like chocolate.

Knows. That's K-N-O-W-S.

Writing 17

Work with your friend. How many sentences can you write?

1. I like writing on the board.
2. Where are you going this weekend?

Joke Corner

34 CD2

What did the snowman say to the other snowman?

"I can smell carrots!"

DIGGORY BONES

36 CD2

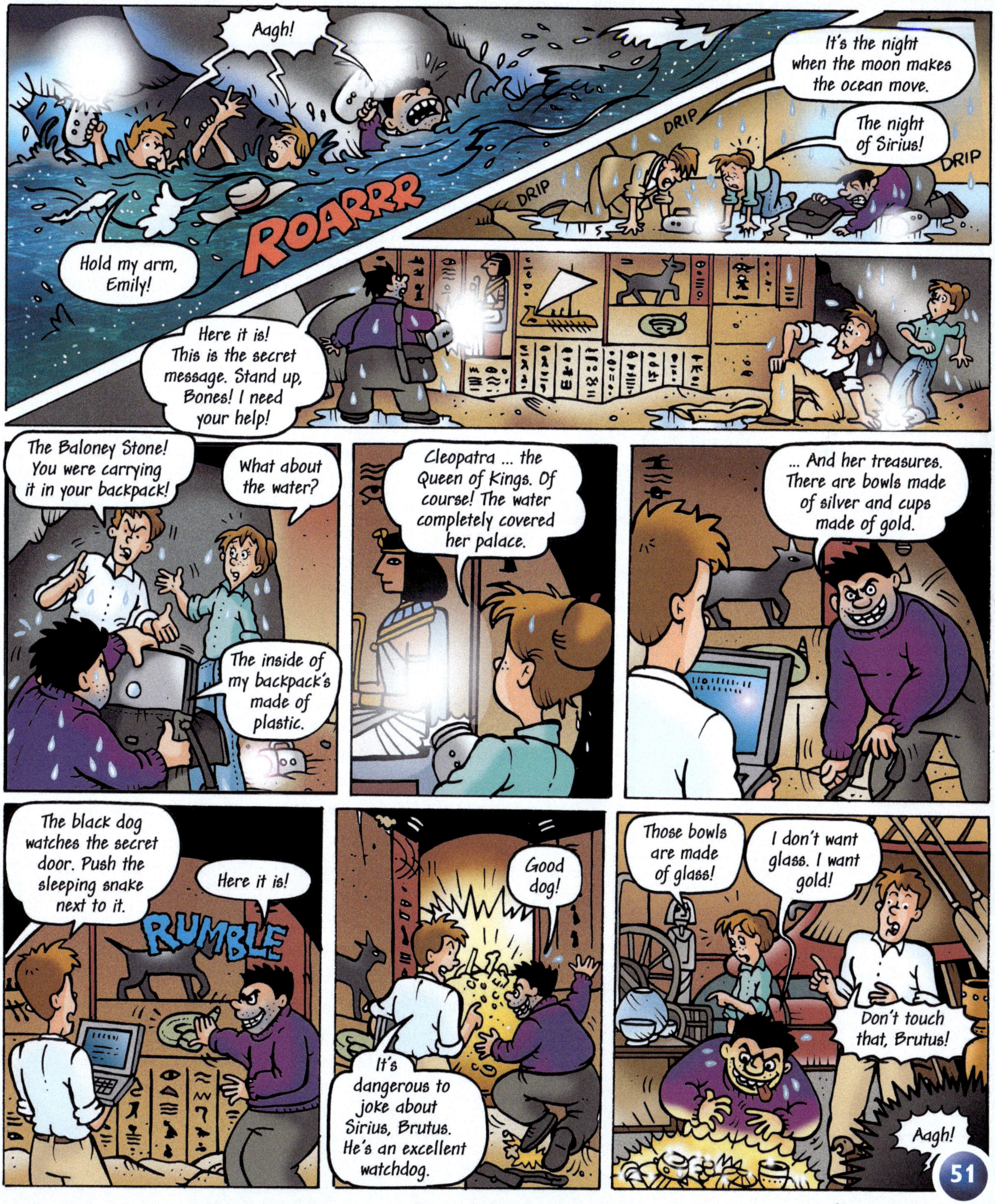

Science Recycling plastic

FACT: **It takes 450 years for plastic bottles to decompose if they are put under the ground.**

1 Read and do.

a) Choose a heading for each paragraph.

- What do we use plastic for?
- Why do we need oil?
- What are some of the different plastics?
- What happens to plastic when we throw it away?

b) Now answer the questions.

2 Read again and choose a title.

a) Different plastics
b) Recycling plastic
c) About plastic

3 37 CD2 Listen and label the diagram.

building	~~bottles and boxes~~	
farming	house	electronics
transportation	other	

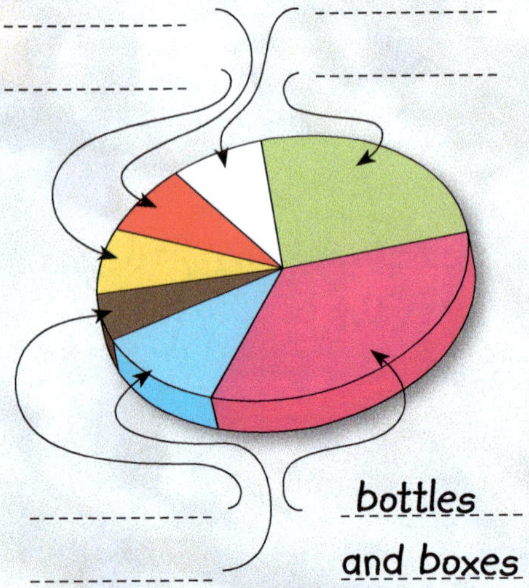

1 ____________________________

Every day we throw a lot of plastic into our garbage cans. This is a problem because plastic does not change. This means that it uses a lot of space if we don't reuse it or recycle it. Did you know that half of the garbage on our beaches is made of plastic?

2 ____________________________

Making plastic also uses a lot of oil. We need to use oil for two things. First, we use it as the basic material for plastic, and second, we use oil for energy to make the plastic. Because of this it is important to try to recycle different plastics. What do you recycle?

3 ____________________________

Celluloid was one of the first plastics. It is made from cotton (the material that jeans are made of) and two other materials. People use celluloid to make film for movies.

Another important plastic is nylon that people use in a lot of different kinds of clothes. The word *nylon* comes from the names of two cities, New York and London.

Today the plastic that we use most is called polyethylene. We use it for bottles and boxes.

4 ____________________________

We use plastic for almost everything. Think about what is around you and what you use every day. How many plastic things can you think of?

4 Read and match.

a

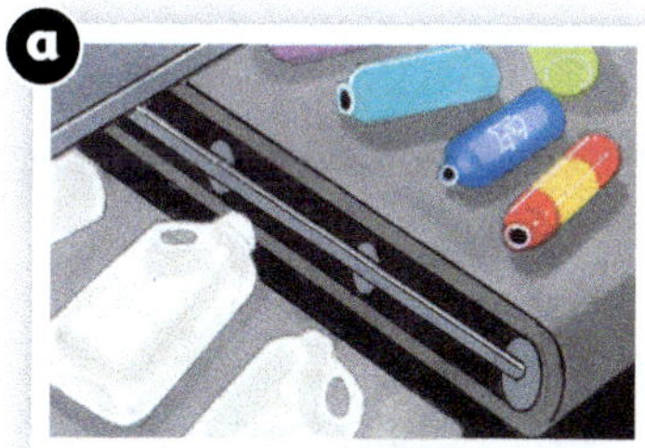

b

c

Recycling plastic

It's not easy to recycle plastic because there are hundreds of different types. How often do you drink from plastic bottles? Here are some of the things people do to recycle them.

1 First, a special machine sorts the bottles so that all of the bottles made from the same materials are together.

2 Then another machine squashes the bottles.

3 Next, another machine cuts the bottles into very small pieces.

4 Then they wash the pieces.

5 Next, they put the plastic into bags, ready for recycling.

6 Finally, they melt the plastic and use it to make a lot of new things. Sometimes they use it to make new plastic bottles!

d

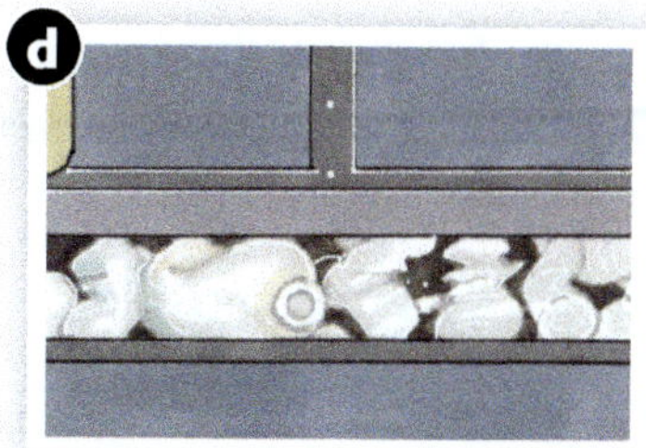

e

f

5 Talk in pairs. Tell the class.

Another thing we can do is reuse our plastic. How can you reuse some of your plastic things?

Project

Make a photo frame.

You need:

- An empty CD box you can reuse
- A picture
- Scissors and glue or tape
- Things to decorate the frame

How to make the photo frame:

1 Open your CD box and take out the paper and the plastic piece where the CD goes.
TIP: Take the cover off the CD box and turn the base on its end. Then put the cover on the back of the base. The box will now stand up on its own.

2 Cut the picture to the right size.

3 Decorate the front of your frame by gluing different objects onto it. You can use stamps, old toys, flowers, or anything you want.

4 Put your picture inside the frame.

6 Senses

Show what you know! What sense words can you remember?

Listening **1** 02 CD3 Listen and check (✓) the sense words you hear.

2 03 CD3 Listen again. Who said it?

1 What does it feel like? (Maria.)
2 It feels like fur.
3 It sounds like somebody falling downstairs.
4 What does this smell like, Maria?
5 It smells like Alex's socks.
6 What does this taste like, Alex?

3 Read and order the words.

1 a / truck. / sounds / My / car / like
2 feels / like / His / jacket / fur.
3 does / taste / What / like? / that / soup
4 your / mother / look / Who / like? / does
5 bananas. / cake / That / smells / like
6 does / your / What / scarf / feel / like?

LOOK

What does it **look/feel/taste/smell/sound** like?
It **looks/feels/tastes/smells/sounds** like coffee.

4 Listen. What does it sound like?

04 CD3

It sounds like a car.

5 Play the game. What does it sound like?

- Think of five things that make different sounds.
- Write the words on five small pieces of paper.
- Give your pieces of paper to your teacher.
- Play the game with the class. Make the sounds and guess.
- Now play the game in groups.

Tick tock tick tock.

It sounds like a clock.

6 Ask and answer. What does it look like?

What do you think number one looks like?

I think it looks like a cat's nose.

So do I.

1 
2 
3 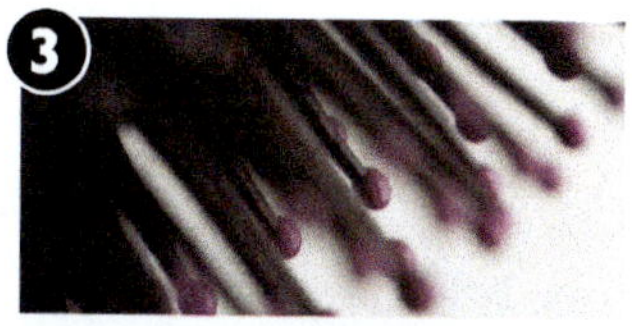
4 
5 
6 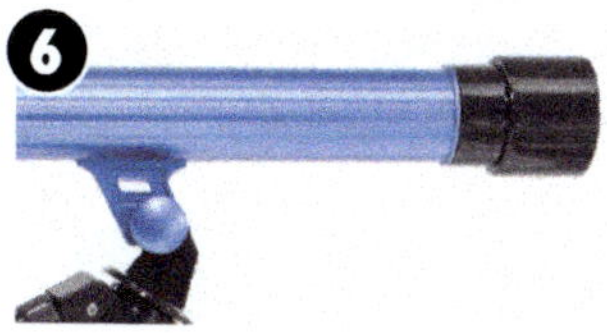
7 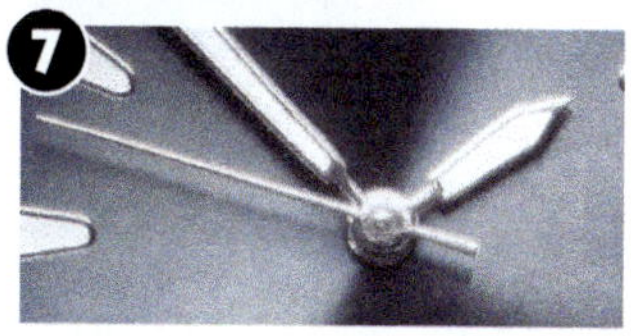
8 

7 Ask and answer. What does it feel like?

What does number one feel like?

It feels soft and furry.

Reading 8 Read and think. What would you put on your pizza?

http://www.cambridge.org/elt/kidsbox/ezine

Kid's Box Ezine!

home | reports | games | world | email

Kid's Box reports Pizza

We wanted to learn how to make pizza, so we went to Luigi's Italian restaurant and spoke to Mario, the cook. Before we started, we washed our hands.

a

First we made the base. The base is made of dough. We put flour, yeast, salt, and water into a bowl, and mixed them well. Then we left the dough for an hour so it could grow.

b

Then we put tomato, cheese, salami sausage, olives, and onion on top of the base. Then we added some black pepper and cooked it in the oven for 15 minutes.

c

When it was ready, we put the pizza onto a plate. Mario uses special plates in the restaurant. They're very big, and they're made of wood.

d

You can eat pizza with your hands, but you need to cut it with a knife first. This one is round, but pizzas can also be square.

e

We had the pizza with salad. We used a big spoon and fork to mix it. Here's a picture of our delicious meal. It looks good, but it tasted even better!

flour | pizza | salt | pepper | knife | fork | spoon | plate

9 (CD3 05) Listen. Repeat the word and find it in the text. 1 Salt. Salt.

10 Read and correct the sentences.

1 Before they started, they washed their feet.
2 They put flour, yeast, salt, and milk into a bowl.
3 They put some black chocolate on top of the pizza.
4 The plates are very big, and they're made of glass.
5 Mario used a spoon to cut the pizza.
6 They mixed the salad with a knife and fork.

11 06 CD3 Listen and match. Check and sing.

My name's Mario,
I'm an Italian cook.
If you want to make a pizza,
Then listen to me and look. e

Take salt, yeast, flour, and water,
Put them in a bowl.
Mix them all together,
And wait for it to grow. ☐

When the base is bigger,
Throw it in the air.
Use your hands to turn it,
Don't get it in your hair. ☐

Now you choose your topping,
Tomato, pepper, and cheese.
You can choose anything,
Sausage, onion, and meat. ☐

Cook for 15 minutes,
Then put it on a plate.
Cut it with a knife and fork,
Mmm. Now that tastes great! ☐

12 08 CD3 Listen and write the words.

1. plate

13 Read and complete. Write the recipe in your notebook.

Ingredients

For the pasta: 

To serve: 

- Put the  onto the table.
- Make a hole in the center of the . Break the  into the hole.
- Mix the  with a . Slowly mix the  with the .
- When you have a ball of dough, mix it with your hands.
- Roll the ball of dough to make it thin. Cut it into long thin pieces with a .
- Put some  in hot water and cook the pasta for about ten minutes.
- Take the pasta out of the water and put it onto a big 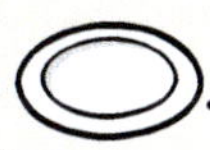.
- Add some , some , and . Mix it with a 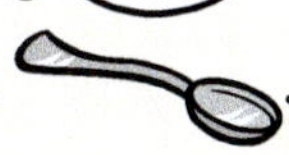.
- Put some black  on top.
- What does it taste like?

14 Focus on phonics

09 CD3

Daisy loves limes, lemons, and plums.
She enjoys music and playing the drums.

Lucy likes rice, salad, and sports.
She also likes science and riding her horse.

Speaking 15 Plan a party. Ask and answer.

You and your friends are going to have a party.
Talk about it. Use these words to ask questions.

Where?	What time / finish?
When?	What / eat?
How many people?	What / drink?
What time / start?	What / need?

Where are we going to have the party?

We can have it at the playground.

Or we can have it in my backyard.

OK.

Writing 16 Write about your plans for the party.

Plan for party
- backyard
- Saturday
- 20

We're going to have the party in my backyard ...

Joke Corner

10 CD3

Why do fish live in salt water?

Because they don't like pepper.

DIGGORY BONES

12 CD3

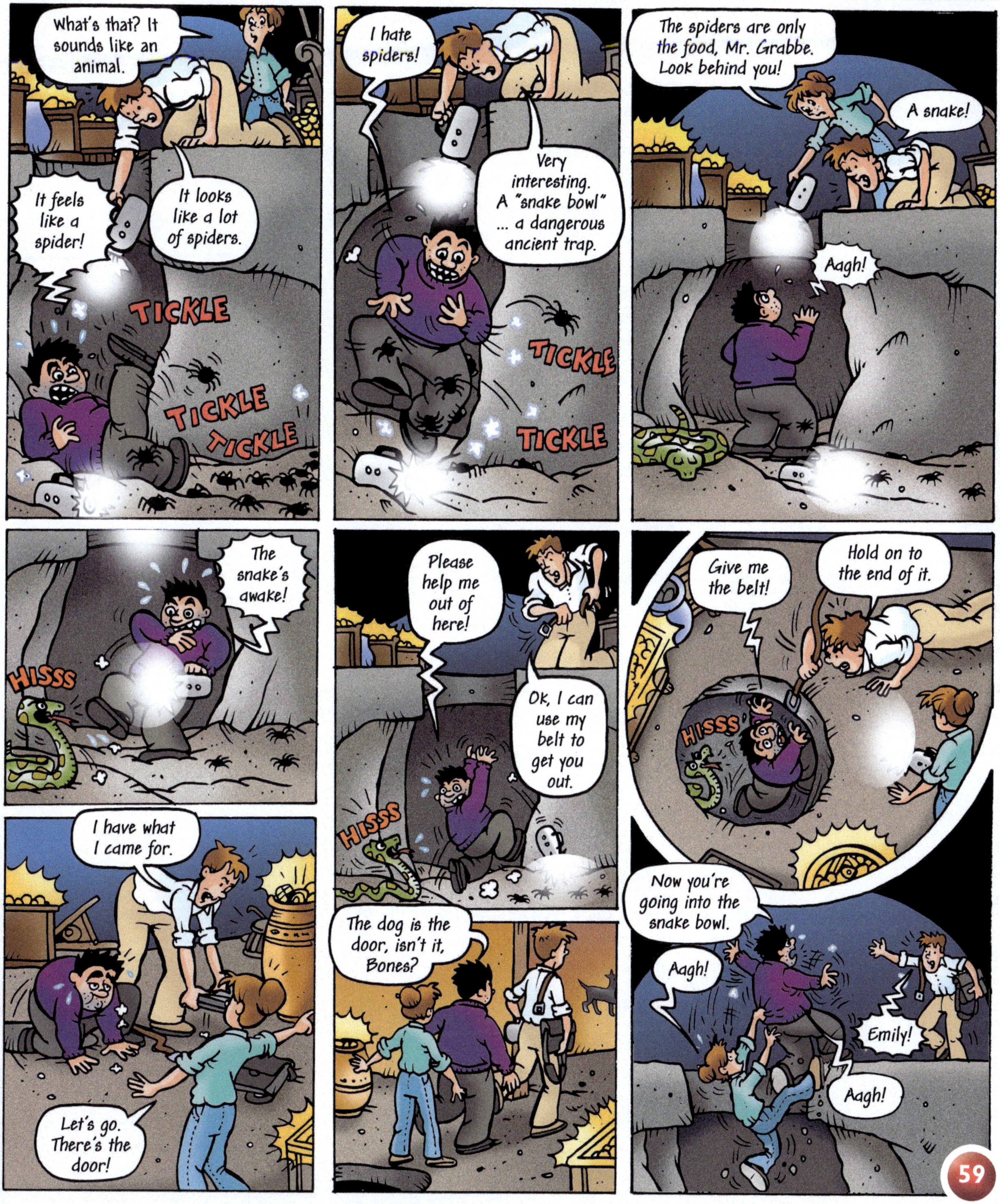

Art Optical illusions

FACT: Our eyes and brain can't always understand everything. How many legs does this elephant have?

1 Look and read. Answer the questions.

When we look at something, light travels from the object to our eye. The eye sends messages to the brain, and the brain tries to understand the message. Because the brain can't understand everything, it tries to make things simpler or easier for us to understand. Some artists play games with this and create amazing paintings and pictures that use "optical illusions." An optical illusion makes us believe we see one thing when really we see something else. It's a great surprise!

Look at these paintings. Which one do you prefer?

Donald Rust painted this picture. It is called *Bison*. Bison are big animals, similar to cows. We can see there are some bison in a field, but when we study the picture more carefully we can find some more.

How many bison are there? Where are they?

This painting is by Salvador Dali and is called *Mae West*. At first sight it looks like a woman's face, but if we look more closely, her face looks like a room with a red wall and a floor that is made of wood. Her hair looks like curtains.

What do her eyes, nose, and mouth look like?

The painting on the right is called *The Human Condition*. It was painted by Rene Magritte. Look at it very carefully.

What can you see?

When we look at it the first time, we think we are looking out of a window, but when we look at it more carefully we can see that there is a painting in front of the window.

What can you see in the painting?

2 Read again and choose a title.

a) Face painting **b)** Understanding pictures **c)** Looking out the window

3 What can you see? Talk in pairs.

a) Julian Beaver drew this picture. He's sitting next to it. How did he draw it? What can you see?

c) Say the color of these words quickly. Do you have any problems? Why?

red blue yellow purple green
yellow blue green red blue
purple green red yellow red
blue purple green red blue
yellow red blue purple red
green yellow purple blue

b) Can you see an old woman or a young woman?

d) Look at this. What can you see? Are the lines straight?

e) Which two animals can you see? Which way are they looking?

Project Make an optical illusion.

You need:

- A pen
- Glue
- White cardboard
- Scissors
- String
- Colored pencils
- A compass

How to make the optical illusion:

1 Draw two circles on the cardboard.

2 Cut the circles out. On one circle, draw and color a piece of cheese. On the other, draw a mouse. Color them in.

3 Glue the circles together. Make one small hole at the top and one at the bottom.

4 Put some string through each hole and make circles with it.

5 Spin the disc quickly and watch the mouse and the cheese. They're in the same place.

Review Units 5 and 6

1 Read the text. Choose the right words and write them on the lines.

Kid's Blog

Hi everyone,

Here are a few lines to tell you about (1) our__________ soccer team. We're (2) ______________ the Springfield Flyers. We (3) ______________ indoor soccer on weekends, and we play against other teams from towns close to ours. There (4) ______________ seven of us on the team. We always change players (5) ______________ only five can play at a time.

(6) ______________ week we played against the team from Fairview. They played really (7) ______________, and they won 4–1. We (8) ______________ the first goal, but then they scored the next four. We're going to win our next game though.

That's all for now,
Robert

1	our	we	us	**5**	but	because	so
2	called	calling	call	**6**	Next	Every	Last
3	plays	playing	play	**7**	well	good	beautiful
4	is	am	are	**8**	marked	scored	do

2 13 CD3 Listen and check (✓) the box.

1 When's David's birthday?

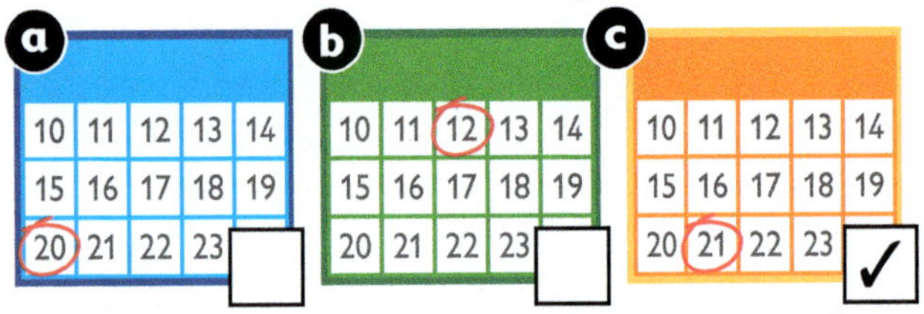

2 What's he going to do on Saturday?

3 What time's the party?

4 Where are they going to go?

5 What was his favorite present last year?

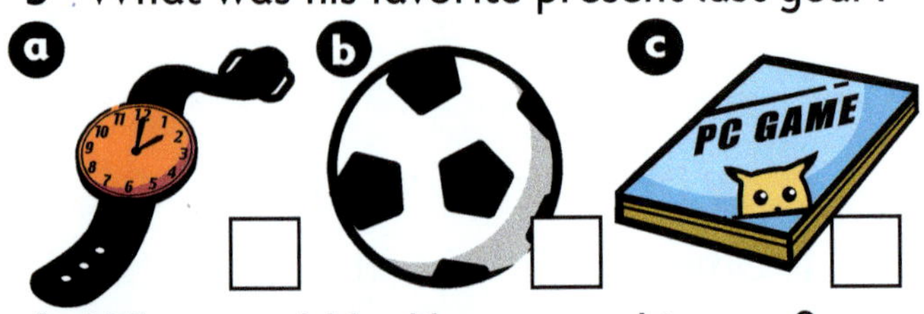

6 What would he like to get this year?

3 Play the game.

Collect the materials

Instructions

- The winner is the first person to get seven things made of different materials.
- Roll the die and move your counter. Say what you can see and what it's made of. If you're right, take another turn. If you're wrong, stop.
- If you stop on something made of a material that you have, miss a turn.

7 Natural world

Show what you know! What nature words can you remember?

Listening **1** 14 CD3 Listen and check (✓) the nature words you hear.

2 15 CD3 Listen again. Say "yes" or "no."

1 They have five days to write their ezine project. (No.)
2 Dan thinks they should put some sunblock on.
3 A man's taking glass bottles and plastic bags out of the lake.
4 He has to do this every day.
5 People should put their garbage in the garbage cans.
6 The kids shouldn't tell their friends about the problem.

LOOK

People **should take** their garbage with them.

They **shouldn't leave** it on the grass.

What **should** we **do** about this?

3 Read and match.

1 It's very hot
2 When the sun is strong
3 We shouldn't leave
4 We should always
5 We shouldn't throw our
6 What should we

a do to help?
b our garbage on the grass.
c garbage into lakes or rivers.
d clean up after a picnic in the country.
e so we should put our hats on.
f we should use sunblock.

4 Listen and complete. Check and sing.

16 CD3

go stop ~~drop~~ jump climb run clean walk put

You shouldn't drop your garbage,
You should ______ it in a garbage can.
You shouldn't leave it on the ground,
You should ______ up everything.
Here comes the bear, here comes the bear!
It's coming for your lunch!

Should I move or should I ______ ?
Should I ______ that tree?
I should do something now.
That bear / cow is after me.

You shouldn't ______ across the field,
You should ______ around.
You shouldn't go too close to that cow,
It can push you to the ground.
You should ______ …
You should ______ quickly!

5 Look and choose the right answer.

1

a) They shouldn't play close to a busy road.
b) They should play carefully.

2

a) He should brush his teeth.
b) He should go to the dentist.

3

a) They should go home.
b) They should wait under a tree.

4

a) They should put their garbage in the garbage can.
b) They shouldn't eat sandwiches outdoors.

5

a) They should walk quietly through the field.
b) They shouldn't go into the field.

6

a) She should wash her hands before she eats.
b) She should wash her hands after she eats.

6 Play the "should" game.

I have an exam tomorrow.

You should go to bed early.

You should study.

You should eat a healthy breakfast.

Reading 7 Read and think. What should you do to help?

http://www.cambridge.org/elt/kidsbox/ezine

Kid's Box Ezine!

home | reports | games | world | email

There are about 1,000 endangered species of animals and birds, and even more species of insects in danger, like butterflies. We should protect them so that they do not become extinct.

Kid's Box reports

Nature Watch

a

b

Two of the world's most famous endangered animals are also famous for their stripes. They are mountain zebras and Siberian tigers. They need big forests to live in, but these forests are smaller nowadays because people cut trees down for wood.

To help protect the tigers in Russia, they made two National Parks. These also protect them from people who want to catch them for their beautiful striped fur.

c

This is the nine-spotted ladybug beetle. It has four black spots on each wing and one in the middle of its body. It lives in North America, and it is an endangered species.

The Lost Ladybug Project asks people to take photos of this beetle if they see it.

d

Frogs are in danger all over the world. The frog in the picture is Lehmann's poison frog. It is found in Colombia. It has red, orange, or yellow stripes.

People named 2008 the "Year of the Frog."

e

Butterflies are beautiful flying insects. This butterfly is the purple spotted butterfly. It has white spots on its purple wings. Every year millions of butterflies fly to a different place. Some die when cars hit them.

In 2007, the Taiwanese government closed a busy highway to protect the purple spotted butterfly!

extinct | wings | spots | spotted | stripes | striped | butterfly | insect | beetle

8 [18 CD3] Listen. Repeat the word and find it in the text. 1 Wings. Wings.

9 Read again and answer.

1 How many endangered species are there?
2 Which animal has red, orange, or yellow stripes?
3 Which animal has a spotted body and wings?
4 Where does the Lehmann's poison frog live?
5 Which animal has white spots on its wings?
6 What did they do to protect butterflies in Taiwan?

10 Look at the pictures. Describe them to your friend.

The female is brown.

The male is more beautiful than the female.

Queen Alexandra's birdwing butterfly

Male

Female

11 Listen. Write words or numbers.

19 CD3

Mary's project

Name of butterfly	1 Queen Alexandra's ____________
Wings measure (Male)	2 ____________ cm
Wings measure (Female)	3 ____________ cm
Description (Female)	4 ____________
Description (Male)	5 ____________

12 Read and complete.

~~thousands~~ should yard butterflies trees extinct

There are (1) *thousands* ____ of endangered species in the world. *Endangered* means there is time to help them before they disappear. They are not (2)________________ . So what should we do? We (3)________________ take care of our world and ask everybody to help make it a cleaner place for animals and insects to live in. We should make ocaens, ponds, streams, and the air much cleaner than they are now … and you can help, too!

You can:

- help clean and protect the habitat in your (4)________________ , close to your house, or on your school ground.
- build homes for animals in (5)________________ .
- plant trees and flowers where insects like (6)________________ can live.
- help projects to plant riverbanks with plants that make the ground stronger and give animals a habitat.

13 Look at the pictures. Talk about what you should do.

I think we should recycle all bottles.

Yes, I agree.

14 Focus on phonics

Spots and **stripes** – **cats** and **dogs**,
Black and **white** – **fish** and **frogs.**
Pink and **green** – **dogs** and **cats**,
Legs and **wings** – **birds** and **bats!**

Speaking 15 Ask and answer.

What should you do?

1 You see someone throwing paper onto the floor. What should you do?
a) Tell them they dropped it. **b)** Do nothing. **c)** Pick it up and recycle it.

2 You see a man making a fire in a field.
a) Do nothing. **b)** Call the fire department. **c)** Tell an adult.

3 You're going to go shopping at the supermarket.
a) Take some old plastic bags. **b)** Buy a lot of candy.
c) Use a lot of plastic bags from the supermarket.

4 You find some money in the street.
a) Put it in your bag. **b)** Take it to the police station. **c)** Do nothing.

5 You see a strange bag on a bus.
a) Tell the bus driver. **b)** Do nothing. **c)** Pick it up.

6 You see a man climbing through the window of the house next door.
a) Do nothing. **b)** Call the police. **c)** Stop and talk to him.

Writing 16 Write your questionnaire.

- Work in pairs and write another questionnaire.
- Think of six problems.
- Think of three possible solutions to each problem.
- Write them out like the ones above.
- Now you can ask your friends the questions.

Joke Corner

Why did the man throw the butter out of the window?

To see the butterfly.

DIGGORY BONES
23 CD3
That wasn't very smart, Brutus.
Run and get help, Dad!
I don't think you should leave your daughter down here with a snake, Bones.
With two snakes, Brutus! One has spots and stripes, but the other doesn't.
HISS
WOOSH
Now there's only one snake ... an ugly, weak one!
Now, Bones, you should turn on the computer for the instructions to get out of here.
You need the instructions to get out of here, but I don't!
You should move slowly and carefully, Emily. This ladder's old, and it isn't very strong.
Ok, Dad.
Wait for me!
The famous butterfly room of Queen Hetepheres! Most people thought this was only a story.
There are thousands of butterflies!
They're all orange and black striped with white spots on their wings.
You shouldn't touch anything, Brutus.
Aagh! Striped insects!
They're the young butterflies! Here are their parents to protect them!

Science Extinction

FACT: Some scientists think that in the last 600 years more than 44,000 different insects have become extinct.

1 Read and answer.

1. Give three reasons animals become extinct.
2. When did the last dinosaurs die?
3. Why did big animals disappear?
4. What did the asteroid do?
5. What happened to the weather?

2 Read again and find words that mean:

1. a family of animals
2. when an animal family dies
3. a big rock from space
4. when the earth moves
5. the opposite of "die"

Extinction

Animals can become extinct when all of their species or family die. When an animal family is in danger of extinction, we call it an endangered species.

A species can become extinct because of many different things:

- more animals eat it
- sudden changes in the weather
- natural disasters
- new diseases
- the actions of people

The most famous extinct animals are the dinosaurs, which died out more than 65 million years ago. People have different ideas about why the dinosaurs became extinct.

Before they disappeared, there was a lot of plate movement. This means that there were volcanic eruptions, earthquakes, tsunamis, and changes in the ocean level. The earth also got colder. These things killed a lot of dinosaurs, but something else happened that killed all animals over 25 kg and a lot of smaller plants and animals.

The most popular idea is that an asteroid, an enormous rock from space, hit the earth and made a big hole. It also started a lot of fires, earthquakes, tsunamis, and storms. The weather became colder, so a lot of plants died. Bigger animals didn't have anything to eat, so they couldn't live.

3 Make a mind map.

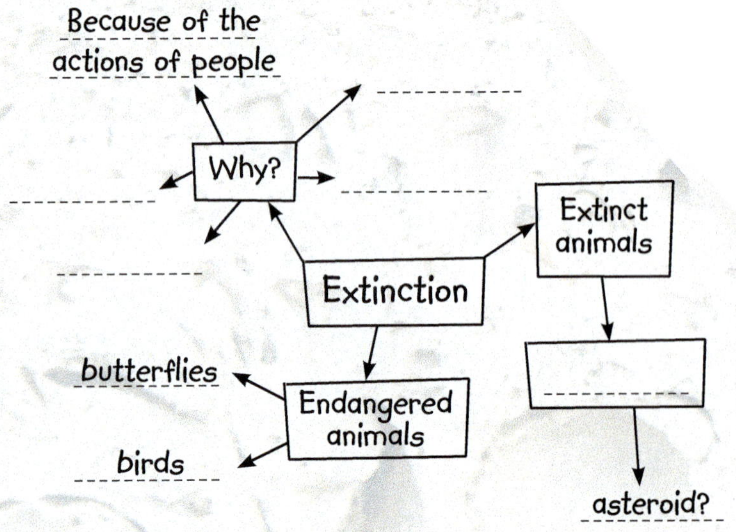

4 Read and match.

a

b

c

d
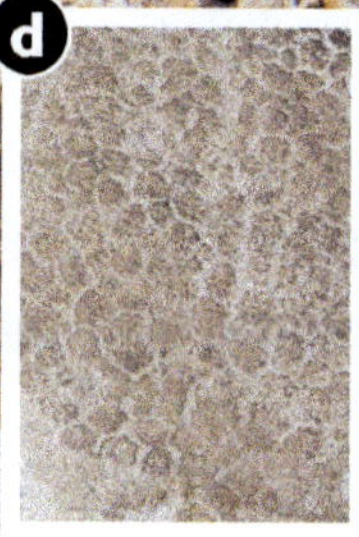

e

We know about dinosaurs because of fossils. Fossils are made from old bones or parts of animals or plants that change into rocks over a very long time. The most important fossils are from parts of the body or from footprints.

Fossils include:

1 Bones: These fossils are the most important when we want to learn about dinosaurs. Archeologists found the first dinosaur bone in 1818 and they find more and more every day.

2 Teeth: These tell us about what different dinosaurs ate.

3 Eggs: Archeologists found the first fossilized dinosaur eggs in France in 1869.

4 Skin: Some dinosaurs had hard thick skin, like crocodiles.

5 Footprints: Dinosaur footprints were normally made in sand. They are important because they tell us about different things, including:

- how big and how fast a dinosaur was
- if the dinosaur walked on two or four legs
- the bones in the dinosaur's foot

5 Find out more.

Are there any dinosaur fossils in your country? See what you can find out.

Project

Make a fossil print.

You need:

- 2 cups of flour
- ½ cup of salt
- ¾ cup of water
- A bowl
- Things to make fossils of (leaves, shells, rocks, cooked and washed chicken leg bones)

How to make your fossil print:

1. Measure and mix together the flour, salt, and water to make a salt dough.
2. Knead the dough for five minutes and make it into balls with your hands.
3. Press your objects into the balls of dough. Make one print in each ball.
4. Put your fossils in a place where they can dry and go hard.

8 World of sports

Show what you know! What sports can you remember?

Listening **1** 25 CD3 Listen and check (✓) the sports words you hear.

2 26 CD3 Listen again. Complete the sentences.

1 Today's the ______________ prize day.
2 Good luck in the race, ______________ .
3 He's ______________ over the sand.
4 He hasn't climbed over the ______________ .
5 He's lost the ______________ .
6 He's stopped to help a ______________ .

3 Read and choose the right words.

1 **We're** / **We've** going to give the prize to the winners of the ezine competition.
2 I've **ever** / **never** won any prizes!
3 **You've** / **You haven't** almost finished!
4 He's **cross** / **crossed** the water.
5 He **haven't** / **hasn't** lost.
6 We've **doing** / **done** it!

LOOK

We**'ve done** it.
He **hasn't lost**.
Have you ever **won** a prize?

4 Choose words to talk about the pictures.

wash	jump	paint	cook	walk	~~start~~

5 Listen and answer the questions.

27 CD3

1 What has she done?
2 What have they done?
3 What has he done?
4 What has Michael done?
5 What have they done?
6 What has Robert done?

6 Read and order the words.

1 this / afternoon. / visited / He's / his / grandmother
2 you / Have / ever / basketball? / played
3 never / ice skating / before. / been / She's
4 He / his / hasn't / done / homework.
5 won / first / We've / prize!
6 entered / the / Have / they / competition?

Reading **7** Read and think. What time of year do people play your favorite sport?

http://www.cambridge.org/elt/kidsbox/ezine

Kid's Box Ezine!

home | reports | games | world | email

When we play some sports, we need the right weather.

Kid's Box reports

Sports for all seasons

a

b

Track and field is a sport that we usually do outside. It's difficult to do in the cold and rain so, in school, we do track and field in the summer. A lot of adults play golf in the summer, but they can play it in the winter, too!

c

d

e

Some sports are only winter sports because we need snow and ice. A lot of people enjoy a winter skiing vacation. Today a lot of young people like snowboarding, too. Sledding is also a lot of fun in the winter. You can sled down a hill.

f

There are other sports that you can play in any season. In England and most of Europe, cycling is a very popular sport. A lot of people cycle in the spring, fall, and winter, not only in the summer. Some people have racing bikes and enter competitions. The most famous bicycle race is the Tour de France, which is in the summer.

The dates for the seasons are different in different parts of the world. In Europe, North America, and Asia, spring is from March to June, but in Australia, Africa, India, and South America, it is from about September to December.

golf | track and field | snowboarding | skiing | sledding | hill | cycling | spring | summer | fall | winter

8 28 CD3 Listen. Repeat the word and say the letter.

1 Skiing.

Skiing. That's "c."

9 Read and correct the sentences.

1 In school they do track and field in the fall.
2 Adults always play golf in the winter.
3 For winter sports we need fog and rain.
4 People go sledding in the summer.
5 The Tour de France is usually in the fall.
6 Spring comes between fall and winter.

10 29 CD3 Listen and write the words.

1. *golf*

11 30 CD3 Listen and order. Check and sing.

a Some like playing soccer,
Some like watching it. ☐

b We've skated in the park,
We've made a ball to throw. ☐

c We've played golf with Grandma,
We've raced against the clock. ☐

d We've skied down a mountain,
We've climbed up a rock, ☐

e **We love sports, swimming, sailing, running!**
We love sports,
We love to do it all. 1

f It's good to move your body,
DON'T JUST SIT! ☐

g We've played badminton and tennis,
We've gone sledding in the snow, ☐

12 Read and complete. Answer the questions.

sledding	skiing	~~mountains~~	hill	snowboarding	snowboard	snowball

This morning Jane is coming home from her vacation in the (1) mountains with her family. She's had a great time. During the week her mother and father went (2) ______________ every morning, but Jane and her older brother Frank went (3) ______________ . After lunch Jane and her brothers played in the snow. They tried to play volleyball with a big (4) ______________ , but it was very difficult because the snow was too soft. On the last day they all went (5) ______________ together. Jane's parents and brothers kept falling and rolling down the (6) ______________ , but Jane was pretty good at it. She wants to buy a (7) ______________ and go to the mountains again next year.

1 Where did Jane go on vacation?
2 Who did she go with?
3 What did her parents do every morning?
4 Which of Jane's brothers went sledding with her?
5 What did they try to play volleyball with?
6 What did they all do on the last day of their vacation?

13 Focus on phonics

32 CD3

Where have they played?
They've played in the sea.
What have they made?
A cup for tea!

What have they bought?
They've bought a dish.
What have they caught?
They've caught a fish!

Speaking 14 Find someone who ...

Have you ever been skiing? — No, I haven't.

Have you ever played golf? — Yes, I have.

Questionnaire

Find someone who ...	Names	
has been skiing.		
has played golf.	Peter	Sally
has won a prize.		
has climbed a mountain.		
has entered a competition.		
has played volleyball.		

Writing 15 Write a report about your class.

I spoke to ten people in my class about
things they have done.
Three of them have been skiing ...

Joke Corner

33 CD3

What do you call a snowball in the summer?

No ball!

DIGGORY BONES
35 CD3
Now what have you done?
You should shut your mouth, Brutus! Those butterflies are dangerous!
The butterflies have started to go back to the walls.
This looks like the way out. It's the first time anyone's used this door.
Wait for me!
TLING TLING
I don't know what's inside, so stay right behind me. Don't try to bring anything with you!
I haven't touched anything.
You need more exercise, Brutus.
The Ancient Egyptians invented field hockey and handball. You should use some of those treasures.
I've waited for this moment all my life ... I'm going to be rich!
When the water comes, swim up to the light.
Right.
BOOOM
Hmm. They've painted sports on these walls ... they're trying to tell us something.
The Ancient Egyptians loved sports.
PUFF
GLOO GLOO
Time to go, Dad!
GURGLE
The Ancient Story of Sirius says you can't take the treasure and live, Brutus.
No! My gold!
I got your email, son. The first one you've ever sent from a snake bowl, huh?
POLICE
Thanks, Dad!
Brutus hasn't come up!
My treasure! I've lost it all!
You're the "treasure" now, Brutus!

Art Olympic design

FACT: The Olympic Games happen every four years. 204 different countries competed in the 2012 Olympics in 26 different sports.

1 Read and match.

1 Can you see the picture with five different colored circles? This is called a logo. It is for the Olympic Games. The circles represent five different continents of the world.

2 Each country also has another logo for its games. The Beijing 2008 logo shows a person dancing. This was the old logo for the city, but it also represents all the different sports at the Olympics.

3 The picture for London plays with the numbers 2012. It is a modern picture, because people wanted young people to watch the games and play more sports.

4 The logo for Rio 2016 shows three people and uses the three colors of Brazil's flag. The shape the people are making looks like Sugarloaf Mountain in Rio. Do you like it?

a

b

c

d

2 Ask and answer.

1 What's a logo?

2 How many circles are there in the Olympic logo? Why?

3 What's the person doing in the Beijing logo?

4 Which city uses numbers in its logo?

5 What colors are used in the Rio logo for 2016? Why?

6 Which is your favorite logo? Why?

Project 1 Design your Olympic logo.

Work in groups. Imagine the next Olympic Games are going to be in your city.

1 Think of a design for a logo.

2 Make a poster to show your design.

3 Show the class and decide on the best logo.

3 Read and answer.

1. How big must the Olympic medals be?
2. How much silver is there in the gold and silver medals?
3. Who is on the front of the Olympic medals?
4. Who decides what goes on the back of the medals?
5. What was on the back of the medals for the Beijing games in 2008?
6. What color is jade?

How are the Olympic medals made?

Each Olympic medal must be at least 68 mm across and 3 mm thick. The gold and silver medals must be at least 92.5% silver. There are six grams of 24-carat gold covering each gold medal. The bronze medals contain a mixture of different metals, including silver.

The front of the medal

Since 1928, there has been a picture of Nike, the Greek goddess of winning, on the front of every medal.

For the 2004 games in Athens, a new front was designed. It had a new picture of Nike flying into the Greek stadium to give the winners their prizes.

The back of the medal

The back of every medal is different for each Olympic Games and is designed by the city where the games are. The medal for the Beijing 2008 Olympic Games had a circle of a green precious stone called jade. Jade is important in China because it means something is beautiful and excellent. The top of the medal looks like a dragon, which shows somebody is strong.

Project 2 Design an Olympic medal.

You need:

- A piece of thin cardboard
- A compass
- A ruler
- A pencil and pens
- Glue
- Scissors
- String or ribbon

How to make your medal:

1. Draw two circles on a piece of thin cardboard. Use a compass to make them exactly 68 mm.
2. Cut out the circles.
3. Draw the goddess Nike on one circle. This is the front of the medal. Then draw your own design for the back of the medal on the other circle.
4. Glue the circles together and use the compass to make a hole at the top.
5. Put string or ribbon through the hole to finish your medal and show it to the class.

Review Units 7 and 8

1 Look at the picture. Talk about it in pairs.

It's a sunny day.

They're outside a restaurant.

Daisy

Sally

Vicky

Fred

John

Paul

Jack

2 36 CD3 Listen and draw lines. There is one example.

3 Read the story. Choose a word from the box. Write the correct word next to numbers 1–5. There is one example.

~~kicked~~	sandwiches	
water	quiet	
have	shouldn't	
are	can	clothes
sand	dangerous	

I went to the beach with Sam and his dad last weekend. We took a picnic and a ball. We were playing soccer on the beach when I *kicked* the ball into the ocean! It was soon far out in the (1) ______________ !

"Can you swim?" Sam asked.

"No, I've never learned to swim!" I answered. "Can you swim?"

"Yes," said Sam, and he started swimming.

The waves were huge.

Sam's dad started shouting at him, "(2) ______________ you seen the flag? You shouldn't swim when there is a red flag!"

Sam's dad swam toward him and pulled him back to the beach.

"Sorry, Dad," Sam said. "The ocean was (3) ______________ !"

"Um. Should we have our picnic, now?" I said.

We went to get our picnic, but it wasn't there.

"You (4) ______________ leave food on the beach!" Sam's dad said. "The birds always eat it. Look!"

It was true. We saw a lot of big white birds eating our (5) ______________ .

Now choose the best name for the story.

Check (✓) one box.

- A day at the beach ☐
- The dangerous birds ☐
- A nice swim ☐

4 Play the game.

What's the question?

Instructions

- Play in pairs. One player is red, and the other is blue. In turns, go around the board. Read the answer and ask the question. If your question is right, score three points. If it's wrong, lose one point. Make a note of the points in your notebook.

Values
Units 1 & 2

Respect in the classroom

1 Look at the picture. What's wrong? Talk to your friends.

Look at "a." What do you think is wrong?

She doesn't have her book for the class.

2 37 CD3 Listen and check. Say the letter.

He's worried because he's late.

That's "d."

3 Ask and answer.

1 What should the children do to start their class on time?
2 Which of the things in the picture do you never do?
3 Which of the things in the picture do you sometimes do?
4 What should you do to be a better student?

People who help us

1 Read and answer the questions.

1 How did Holly break her leg? 2 Why did she hit her head? 3 Who helped her?

Holly's heroes

It's a rainy day, and there are gray clouds in the sky. Holly's walking to school. She has a history exam. A lot of young people might feel unhappy or worried, but not Holly. Holly's just happy she can walk to school.

Last year Holly was in the hospital for four weeks, and she had to learn to walk again. We ask Holly about her heroes.

So, Holly, can you tell us what happened to you last year?

I was cycling home from my friend's house after school. It was dark, and I didn't have any lights, so I couldn't see clearly. I was going very quickly down a hill when suddenly a cat ran across the road in front of me. I tried not to hit it, but I fell off my bike.

How terrible! Then what happened?

Well, I can't remember. I hit my head because I wasn't wearing a helmet. People told me what happened. I fell badly and broke my leg in two places.

How did you get to the hospital?

A driver saw me on the ground and stopped his car. He called for an ambulance, and they took me to the closest hospital. I arrived in less than ten minutes.

Wow! That was fast.

Yes. Thanks to them, the doctors and nurses could work quickly. I had an X-ray, and then they had to operate for four hours, but they saved my leg. Then I had to learn to walk again.

So you have a lot of heroes: the ambulance drivers and the team of doctors and nurses.

Yes, but also the driver who stopped to call the ambulance. I want to say thank you to everyone who helped me. When I grow up, I want to be a doctor or nurse because I'd like to help other people, too.

2 38 CD3 Listen and say "firefighter," "doctor," "police officer," or "ambulance driver."

Values
Units 5 & 6

Tell the truth but don't hurt

1 Read and choose answers.

1 **Your friend has a new haircut, and you think it looks awful. When he asks you what you think, you say:**

a) "It looks terrible. I don't like it."
b) "It's OK, but I prefer the old haircut."
c) "It looks amazing! It's perfect for you."

2 **Your mom spent all afternoon making a special dinner, but you don't like it. What do you do?**

a) You eat it and ask for more.
b) You make a horrible face and say you don't want to eat it.
c) You tell her that it's nice, but it's not your favorite meal. Suggest a meal that she can make more quickly and easily.

3 **You're shopping with a friend who wants to buy a new dress. She tries on a dress that looks awful on her. She asks you what you think. What do you do?**

a) You say the dress doesn't look very nice, and you find a different dress for her to try.
b) You say that the dress looks nice and tell her to buy it.
c) You tell her the dress looks horrible and you're bored with shopping.

4 **A new boy in your class invites you to play tennis on Saturday afternoon. You'd like to go to the movies with some friends. What do you do?**

a) You say, "Sorry, I can't. I want to go to the movies with my friends."
b) You make a horrible face and say, "I hate tennis!"
c) You smile and say, "Thanks very much, but I want to go to the movies with some friends on Saturday. Would you like to come with us?"

5 **You have a friend who sometimes smells bad after his tennis lesson. What's the best way to help him?**

a) Make a horrible face and say, "You smell bad. Take a shower!"
b) Give him a box of shower gel and deodorant for his birthday.
c) Talk about him with the other students and laugh.

6 **Your dad doesn't have a job. He lost it last year, and your parents are worried about money. It's your birthday soon, and you want a big party, but your parents say that you can't have one this year. What do you do?**

a) You tell your parents that you understand and it isn't important.
b) You get angry and stay in your room all day.
c) You tell your parents that you understand. You ask your friends to bring some lemonade and chips to the park so you can have a small party.

2 Talk about your answers with your friend. Are they the same or different?

3 Discuss these questions.

1 Is it important to always tell the truth?
2 Are there some situations where it's OK not to tell the truth?
3 How can we say things to help our friends and not hurt their feelings?

Value your friendships

1 Read the letters and answer the questions.

Dear Betty and Robert,

I work really hard at school and I always study a lot for my exams, but I don't get good marks. I don't fail, but I get 5, 6, or sometimes 7 out of 10.

My best friend, Emma, gets the best marks in the school, but she cheats. She takes pictures of the book on her cell phone and uses them in the exams. I'm really unhappy about this.

Should I do the same as my friend and get better marks or should I tell the teacher that she cheats in exams? Please help me decide.

Yours,

Richard

1 Does Richard work hard at school?
2 Does he get good marks?
3 How does Emma cheat in the exams?

Dear Richard,

When you work hard at school and study for your exams, you are learning things. I'm sorry that you don't get the good marks that you want. It's better to work hard and learn things than cheat and learn very little. It's not a good idea for you to do the same as Emma. You should feel good because you're passing your exams. Do your best and don't worry about other people's marks.

This situation is difficult. You don't have to tell the teacher that your friend is cheating. Emma can't always cheat – one day someone is going to catch her.

Yours,

Betty and Robert

4 What do Betty and Robert think about cheating?
5 Do they think that Richard should get the same marks as other students?

2 Discuss these questions.

1 Is Sarah right to be unhappy? Why?
2 What do you think Katy should do?
3 What do you think Sarah should do?

Dear Betty and Robert,

I'm really unhappy because I've made a huge mistake with my best friend, Sarah. There's a group of very popular girls in my class. They're cool and funny, and everyone wants to be friends with them. They asked me to go out with them last Saturday. I was really excited, but it was Sarah's birthday.

I didn't go to Sarah's party, and now she's unhappy with me. Now she doesn't want to be my friend. I've started to see that the popular girls are boring and unkind, and I don't like going out with them. I want to be Sarah's best friend again. What should I do?

Yours,

Katy

Grammar reference

1

What time is it?

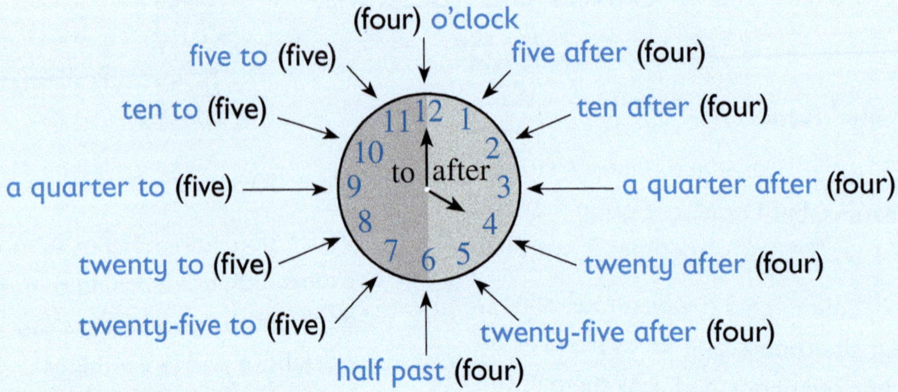

2

We use *going to* to talk and write about the future.

Affirmative	**Negative (n't = not)**	**Question**
I'm going to work hard.	I'm not going to work hard.	Am I going to work hard?
She's going to work hard.	She isn't going to work hard.	Is she going to work hard?
They're going to work hard.	They aren't going to work hard.	Are they going to work hard?

3

right	She turned right.
left	They took the second street on the left.
across	They looked and listened carefully before they walked across the street.
down	We walked down the street.
straight ahead	He didn't turn. He drove straight ahead to the end of the road.
corner	I turned at the corner.
past	You have to walk past the park.

4

We use the past progressive to describe what was happening in the past.

Affirmative	Negative (n't = not)	Question
I was reading a book.	I wasn't reading a book.	Was I reading a book?
We were reading a book.	We weren't reading a book.	Were we reading a book?

5

We use *made of* to describe materials.

Affirmative	Negative (n't = not)	Question
It's made of metal.	It isn't made of metal.	Is it made of metal?
They're made of metal.	They aren't made of metal.	Are they made of metal?

6

We use verb + *like* to describe things.

Affirmative	Negative (n't = not)	Question
It sounds like a train.	It doesn't sound like a train.	Does it sound like a train?
They sound like cats.	They don't sound like cats.	Do they sound like cats?

7

We use *should* to give and ask for help or advice.

Affirmative	Negative (n't = not)	Question
I should tell my teacher.	I shouldn't tell my teacher.	Should I tell my teacher?
He should tell his teacher.	He shouldn't tell his teacher.	Should he tell his teacher?

8

We use the *present perfect* to talk and write about things we did any time up to now.

Affirmative	Negative (n't = not)	Question
They've visited London.	They haven't visited London.	Have they visited London?
She's visited London.	She hasn't visited London.	Has she visited London?

Thanks and Acknowledgments

Authors' thanks

Many thanks to everyone at Cambridge University Press and in particular to:

Rosemary Bradley, for overseeing the whole project and successfully pulling it all together with good humor;
Fiona Davis, for her fine editorial skills;
Colin Sage for his good ideas and helpful suggestions;
Karen Elliott for her enthusiasm and creative reworking of the Phonics sections.

We would also like to thank all our students and colleagues at Star English, El Palmar, Murcia, and especially Jim Kelly and Julie Woodman for their help and suggestions at various stages of the project.

Dedications

For Carmen Navarro with love. Many thanks for all your hard work, help, and support over the years – CN

To my Murcian family: Adolfo and Isabel, the Peinado sisters and their other halves for always treating me so well, Thanks for being there and for making my life in Murcia so much fun – MT

The authors and publishers would like to thank the following teachers for their help in reviewing the material and for the invaluable feedback they provided:

Rocío Licea Ayala, Natalia Bitar, Diego Andres Gil Chibuque, Gayane Grigoryan, Shaun Sheahan, Gicela Ugalde.

We would also like to thank all the teachers who allowed us to observe their classes and who gave up their invaluable time for interviews and focus groups.

The authors and publishers acknowledge the following sources of copyright material and are grateful for the permissions granted. While every effort has been made, it has not always been possible to identify the sources of all the material used or to trace all copyright holders. If any omissions are brought to our notice, we will be happy to include the appropriate acknowledgments on reprinting.

p.6(a,b,c): © Stephen Bond; p.6(d): Alamy/© Lennello Calvetti; p.6(e): Shutterstock/© Titov Dmitry; p.6(f): Alamy/© Steve Vidler; p.11: © Stephen Bond; p.12(a): Rex Features/ © Universal/Everett; p.12(b): Rex Features/© Steve Meddle; p.12(c): Alamy/© Image Source; p.12(d): Shutterstock/© Nazarino; p.12(e): Shutterstock/© Florian Ispas; p.12(f): Rex Features/© Roderick Barker-Benfield; p.12(f): Getty Images/© AFP: p.12(g): Shutterstock/© Pavel Shchegolev; p.13(1): Rex Features/© Steve Meddle; p.13(2): Alamy/© Peter Phipp/Travelshots.com; p.13(3): Alamy/© Image Source; p.13(4): Corbis/© David Spurdens; p.16(background): Shutterstock/© Mhatzapa; p.16(T): Rex Features/© 20th Century Fox/Everett; p.16(a): Alamy/© AF Archive; p.16(b): Rex Features/© Everett Collection; p.16(c): Kobal Collection/© Universal; p.16(BL): Alamy/© Megapress; p.16(C): Corbis/© Sergio Gaudenti/Kipa; p.16(CR): Getty Images/© Time & Life Pictures; p.16(BR): Corbis/© Louis Quail/ In Pictures; p.17(TR): Topfoto; p.17(TL): Rex Features/© Everett Collection; p.17(CR): Kobal Collection/© Dreamworks LLC; p.17(B): © Stephen Bond; p.20(a): Rex Features/© Stewart Cook; p.20(b): Alamy/© CBW; p.20(c): Getty Images/ p.20(d): Rex Features/© Julian Makey; p.20(e): Alamy/Kolvenbach; p.20(f): Shutterstock/© BrAt82; p.22: © Stephen Bond; p.24(background): Shutterstock/© Trendywest; p.24(T): © The Museum of London; p.24(TR): Shutterstock/© Vipman; p.24(a): Shutterstock/© Pressmaster; p.24(b): Alamy/© Henry E Iddon; p.24(c): Alamy/© Moodboard; p.25(TR):Alamy/© YAY Media AS; p.25: © Stephen Bond; p.30(a): Alamy/© Steve Vidler; p.30(b): Alamy/© Jack Sullivan; p.30(c): Alamy/© Bob Masters; p.30(d): Alamy/© Andrew Holt; p.30(e): Alamy/© Geoff A Howard; p.30(f): Alamy/© Anthony Kay/Loop Images; p.30(g): Shutterstock/© Justin Black; p.30(h): Shutterstock/© Kamira; p.34(background): Shutterstock/© Yunjun; p.34(a): Shutterstock/© Viacheslav Lopatin; p.34(b): Shutterstock/© Stuart Monk; p.34(c): Alamy/© Sean Pavone; p.34(d): Shutterstock/© Upthebanner; p.34(BR): Alamy/© UIG/DeAgnosti; p.35: © Stephen Bond; p.38(a): Corbis/© Bettmann ; p.38(b): Alamy/© GL Archive; p.38(c): Corbis/© Daniel Aguiler; p.38(d): Shutterstock/© Warren Goldswain; p.38(e): Getty Images; p.38(f): Shutterstock/© Barry Tuck; p.39: © Stephen Bond; p.42(background): Getty Images/© Digital Vision; p.42(T): Corbis/© Andrew Cowin/Travel Ink; p.43: © Stephen Bond; p.44(TR): Shutterstock/© Naipung; p.44(L): Alamy/© Howard Barlow; p.44(R): Bridgeman Art Library/© Private Collection; p.47(a): Alamy/© Anna Stowe; p.47(b): Shutterstock/© Blazej Lyjak; p.47(c): Shutterstock/© Mrsiraphol; p.47(d): Alamy/© O. Digoit; p.47(e): Alamy/© Anton Starikov; p.47(f): Shutterstock/© Smith; p.47(g): Alamy/© Mira; p.47(h): Shutterstock/© Karkas; p.48(a): Used with kind permission of Réjeanne Arsenault; p.48(b): Press Association/© Rajanish Kakade/AP; p.48(c): Alamy/© K-Photos; p.48(d); Getty Images/© AFP; p.48(e): © Trustees of the British Museum; p.48(f): Shutterstock/© Blanscape; p.49: © Stephen Bond; p.52(background): Shutterstock/© Bogdan Ionescu; p.52(T): Shutterstock/© Pics Five; p.52(TR): Getty Images; p.52(CL): Shutterstock/© Flasioo; p.52(CR): Shutterstock/© Elnur; p.52(B): Shutterstock/© Huyangshu; p.53: © Stephen Bond; p.55(TR): © Stephen Bond; p.55(1): Shutterstock/© Bofotolux; p.55(2,3): © Stephen Bond; p.55(4): Shutterstock/© Yeko Photo Studio; p.55(5): Shutterstock/© Tamara Kulikova; p.55(6): Shutterstock/© Trekandshoot; p.55(7): Shutterstock/© Anteromite; p.55(8): Shutterstock/© Berislav Kovacevic; p.55(B): © Stephen Bond; p.56(ALL): © Stephen Bond; p.60(background): Superstock/© Ingram Publishing; p.60(TR): © Donald Rust; p.60(L): © Salvador Dali, Gala-Salvador Dali Foundation DACS, London 2009; p.60(BR): © National Gallery of Art, Washington DC, USA/Lauros/ Giraudon/The Bridgeman Art Library, ©ADAGP, Paris and DACS, London 2009; p.61(TL): Alamy/© Justin Kase z11z;l p.61(CL): Corbis/ Swim Inc 2m, LLC: p.61(C): © DK Images; p.61(B): © Stephen Bond; p.63(wool hat): Shutterstock/© Lucy Liu; p.63(bread): Shutterstock/© Anna Breitenberger; p.63(doll): Alamy/© D Hurst; p.63(earrings): Shutterstock/© Africa Studio; p.63(window): Shutterstock/© Pavels; p.63(airplane): Shutterstock/© Ugorenkov Aleksandr; p.63(toy car): Alamy/© Emmanuel Lattes: p.63(door): Shutterstock/© Scorpp; p.63(belt): Shutterstock/© SS1001; p.63(robot): Getty Images/© CSA Plastok; p.63(scarf): Shutterstock/© Adisa; p.63(knife): Shutterstock/© Tischenko Irina; p.63(notebook): Shutterstock/© Theeradech Sanin; p.63(mirror): Shutterstock/© James Steidl; p.63(cake): Shutterstock/© Noonday; p.63(bag): Shutterstock/© M Unal Ozmen; p.63(trophy): Shutterstock/© Boris Rabtsevich; p.63(box): Shutterstock/© RT Images; p.63(ring): Shutterstock/© Johnny Lye; p.63(bike): Shutterstock/© Horiyan; p.63(cup): Shutterstock/© Danny Smythe; p.63(eraser): Shutterstock/© PicsFive; p.63(bin bag): Shutterstock/© Hans Slegers; p.63(bottle): Shutterstock/© Anaken 2012; p.63(jumper): Shutterstock/© Chamille White; p.63(shoes): Shutterstock/© Patricia Hofmeester; p.63(paper bag): Shutterstock/© Naypong; p.63(silver bracelet): Getty Images/iStock/ppart; p.63(toy train): Shutterstock/© VHdtlm; p.63(chair): Shutterstock/© Photobac; p.763(truck): Alamy/© Gabe Palmer; p.63(comic): Alamy/© Boy Kyrpos; p.63(spoon): Shutterstock/© Stephen Rees; p.63(pizza): Shutterstock/© Kesu; p.63(watch): Shutterstock/© Maraze; p.63(glass): Shutterstock/© Mariyana M; p.66(a): Shutterstock/© Eco Print; p.66(b): Shutterstock/© Andrey Khrolenok; p.66(c): Getty Images/EyeEm/Ahmed Nooh; p.66(d): Ardea/© Thomas Marent; p.66(e): Alamy/© Danita Delimont; p.67(ALL): Nature Picture Library/© Bristol City Museum; p.70(background): Shutterstock/© Sergiy Artsaba; p.70(T): Getty Images/© Stocktrek Images; p.70(B): Corbis/© Mike Agliolo; p.71(a): Alamy/© Hoberman Collection; p.71(b): Science Photo Library/© Sinclair Stammers; p.71(c): Corbis/© Reuters; p.71(d): Getty Images/© Ken Lucas/ Visuals Unlimited; p.71(e): Corbis/© Louie Psihoyos; p.71: © Stephen Bond; p.74(a): Alamy/© Janine Weidel Photo Library; p.74(b): Alamy/© INDASCO Photography; p.74(c): Getty Image/© Scott Markewitz; p.74(d): Corbis/© David Spurdons; p.74(e): Alamy/© Kuttig-People; p.74(f): Getty Images/Lonely Planet Images/Angus Oborn; p.78(background): Shutterstock/ Andrey Armyagov; p.78(TR): Rex Features/© Brice Adams/Daily Mail; p.78(a): Alamy/© One-Image Photography; p.78(b): Alamy/© Grzegory Knec; p.78(c,d): Alamy/© Concept Media; p.78: © Stephen Bond; p.79(L, R): Rex Features/© Top Photo Group; p.79(c): Alamy/© Image Broker; p.79: © Stephen Bond; p.83: Shutterstock/© Monkey Business Images.

The authors and publishers are grateful to the following illustrators:

FLP; Graham Kennedy; Gywneth Williamson; Jo Taylor, c/o Sylvie Poggio; John Woodcock, c/o Thorogood kids; Lisa Smith, c/o Sylvie Poggio; Melanie Sharp, c/o Sylvie Poggio; Moreno Chiacchiera, c/o Beehive; Teresa Tibbetts, c/o Beehive; Ken Oliver, c/o Art agency; Christian Cornia, c/o Advocate Art; Alan Rowe

The publishers are grateful to the following contributors:

Stephen Bond: commissioned photography
Alison Prior: picture research
Wild Apple Design Ltd: page design
Lon Chan: cover design
Jo Taylor: cover illustration
John Green and Tim Woolf, TEFL Audio: audio recordings
Songs written and produced by Robert Lee, Dib Dib Dub studios.
John Marshall Media, Inc. and Lisa Hutchins: audio recordings for the American English edition
hyphen S.A.: publishing management, American English edition